# Creating High-Performance
# Government Organizations

Alliance for Redesigning Government

Mark G. Popovich, *Editor*

*Foreword by* David Osborne

# Creating High-Performance Government Organizations

## A Practical Guide for Public Managers

*Writing Team:*
Jack A. Brizius, Gail C. Christopher,
Barbara R. Dyer, Susan E. Foster,
Martha G. Miller, Mark G. Popovich,
Susan Resnick-West

JOSSEY-BASS
A Wiley Imprint
www.josseybass.com

Jossey-Bass books and products are available through most bookstores. To contact Jossey-Bass directly, call (888) 378-2537, fax to (800) 605-2665, or visit our website at www.josseybass.com.

Substantial discounts on bulk quantities of Jossey-Bass books are available to corporations, professional associations, and other organizations. For details and discount information, contact the special sales department at Jossey-Bass.

We at Jossey-Bass strive to use the most environmentally sensitive paper stocks available to us. Our publications are printed on acid-free recycled stock whenever possible, and our paper always meets or exceeds minimum GPO and EPA requirements.

**Library of Congress Cataloging-in-Publication Data**

Creating high-performance government organizations : a practical guide
  for public managers / Mark G. Popovich, editor ; foreword by David
  Osborne ; writing team, Jack A. Brizius, ... [et al.]. — 1st ed.
      p.   cm. — (The Jossey-Bass nonprofit and public management
series)
  Includes bibliographical references and index.
  ISBN 0-7879-4102-6
  1. Organizational change.   2. Public administration.
I. Popovich, Mark G.   II. Brizius, Jack A.   III. Series.
JF1525.O73C74   1998
  352.3'67—dc21                                           97-52364

The Jossey-Bass
Nonprofit and Public Management Series

# Contents

*To the people in the trenches of organizational change and innovation who are a constant inspiration—and to the memory of Jack Brizius*

# —— Foreword

In the six years since Ted Gaebler and I published *Reinventing Government,* much has changed in the public sector. The Clinton administration has launched its National Performance Review, spurring profound improvements in dozens of federal agencies. Congress has passed two major procurement reform bills and the Government Performance and Results Act, which required federal agencies to do strategic planning and measure their performance.

From Richmond and Charlotte in the South to Minneapolis and Milwaukee in the Midwest to San Diego, Seattle, and Portland in the West, dozens of large cities have embarked on reinvention. Big-city police departments in New York, Boston, and elsewhere have begun measuring results, decentralizing authority, and working in partnership with the community. Crime rates have plummeted. Indianapolis, Philadelphia, Cleveland, and many other cities have embraced competition between public and private service providers.

Hundreds of smaller cities and counties have pursued less publicized but often more profound transformations of their own. School districts have continued their decade-long push for change, spurred on by a rapidly expanding charter school movement. And at the state level, perhaps half the states—led by Florida, Oregon, Iowa, Ohio, Utah, Arizona, Minnesota, Michigan, Wisconsin, and Texas—have launched serious reinvention efforts of one kind or another.

Ideas that were considered new and foreign six years ago are now commonplace: the importance of getting clear on each organization's mission; the practice of measuring performance and creating consequences; the notion of listening to one's customers; the idea of empowering front-line employees and flattening hierarchies; the concept of community-oriented policing; the practice of public versus private competition. When we first wrote about these ideas, many of them were loudly rejected by critics as inappropriate for public institutions. Today they are well within the mainstream.

And yet, whenever I work as a consultant with local, state, or federal organizations, I am struck by how difficult this transition from twentieth-century bureaucracies to twenty-first century governance is for people. On a day-to-day basis, it is confusing, confounding, and enormously frustrating. Change agents hit roadblocks constantly, and political champions frequently move on before the job is complete.

Because there are no road maps guiding this great migration from one form of organization to another, Peter Plastrik and I published *Banishing Bureaucracy* in 1997. It describes the strategies that reinventors around the globe—from New Zealand to the United Kingdom to the United States—have found to be the most successful. Yet many of those who are trying to follow the paths laid down by these pioneers need even more detailed maps. Indeed, I am often asked for a kind of cookbook, a step-by-step recipe for reinvention.

There is no such thing, and given the diversity of public institutions and political environments, there never will be. But with this handbook, my colleagues at the Alliance for Redesigning Government have begun to lay down some concrete steps reinventors can use to transform their organizations. They have focused primarily on the approach Plastrik and I call performance management: the development of long-term outcome goals, performance measures, and performance indicators at all levels of the organization, followed by the creation of rewards and consequences for performance.

If you choose to use this approach—as more and more public organizations have—this book will help you understand what preconditions you will need (such as "consistent, sustained leadership"), how to get started (by "clarifying your purpose, understanding your environment, engaging stakeholders, and building commitment to change"), what steps you will need to take along the way, and how to manage the politics of change.

Perhaps the greatest contribution the authors make is to insist that in working to create a high-performance organization you must change everything about the organization: not just its work processes or how it is structured but its relationship with its customers, its culture, and even its administrative systems. In three particularly valuable chapters, the authors describe how and why you will need to change your budget, human resources, and procurement systems to create high-performance, twenty-first century organizations.

Reinvention is not a linear, predictable process, as the authors make clear. No book can offer the last word on how to create high-performance organizations. Some who read this book will no doubt make their own contributions to the literature based on lessons learned while implementing their own transformation processes. But if you seek wisdom about the bases you will need to cover in order to reinvent your organization, you will find much here.

When Neal Peirce, Scott Fosler, Barbara Dyer, and I created the Alliance for Redesigning Government in early 1993, we hoped to create a network through which thousands of practitioners struggling at the frontiers of reinvention could learn from one another. This volume, the Alliance's second book, is the outcome of listening to and working with those practitioners. We hope you find it a useful contribution, and we hope you will join the conversation that produces such books by joining the Alliance.

*Essex, Massachusetts*                                              DAVID OSBORNE
*December 1997*

# ——ᴍᴍ— Acknowledgments

We developed this book as a practical guide that people from all levels of public sector organizations can use as they seek constantly to improve their organization's performance. The book was motivated by our belief that doing the public's work, whether at the federal, state, or local level, is a high calling. It is important work precisely because it has such a direct impact on the day-to-day lives and the futures of people, families, and communities. We are inspired by the countless public servants who work every day with almost limitless dedication and entrepreneurial energies. They are making a difference for all of us.

David Osborne and Ted Gaebler, through their book *Reinventing Government,* set the course for change in 1992. Their book provided a name for a movement already under way in government. Their ideas have defined a pathway and challenged innovators across the public sector. President Bill Clinton and Vice President Al Gore harnessed their ideas and those drawn from others to improve performance in federal agencies. But equally or even more impressive efforts were launched by elected and appointed leaders, agency heads, managers, and front-line workers at the local and state levels. They have all inspired us through this task. And we have drawn on some of their stories to solidly ground the ideas that are at the heart of this book.

The Alliance for Redesigning Government of the National Academy of Public Administration was the genesis for this project. As a home base, the alliance and the academy have always been supportive, challenging, and constructive. The ideas for this project grew from Barbara Dyer's fertile imagination. She was a cofounder and the executive director through the alliance's first three and one-half years. Dyer was our constant champion—and demanding task master.

But even the best ideas remain on the drawing boards without the resources to bring them to life. The generous support of both The Ford Foundation (Michael Lipsky, senior program officer) and The Pew Charitable Trusts (Tamar Datan, program officer) made this project possible. We greatly appreciate their patience and encouragement.

A working group guided and helped shape this book from its inception. Members of the group included Karen Alderman, U.S. Department of Defense; Aida Alvarez, Office of Federal Housing Enterprise Oversight; Susan Cohen, University of Southern California; Robert Denhardt, University of Central Florida; Dianna Durham-McLoud, Illinois Department of Public Aid; Ken Farrell, The Farrell Group; R. Scott Fosler, National Academy of Public Administration (NAPA); Mary Ann Von Glinow, Florida International University; Dick Gross, Council of Governors' Policy Advisors; William Hudnut, The Hudson Institute; Michelle Hunt, Federal Quality Institute; Donovan King and Bob McGarrah, American Federation of State, County, and Municipal Employees (AFSCME); Nancy Mills, Service Employees International Union; Almella Starks, Federal Express; and Peter Szanton, Szanton Associates.

In addition to the working group, reviewers told us clearly where we were wrong, where we were right, and how we could improve the book. The reviewers included Frank Cipolla, NAPA; Jack Denzlow, U.S. Department of Defense; Sandy Hale, Enterprises Management; David Hoffman, American Federation of Labor and Congress of Industrial Organizations; Ron Jansen, Phoenix Public Works Director; Grantland Johnson, U.S. Department of Health and Human Services; John Kaminsky, National Performance Review; Scott Livingston, attorney with the law firm of Rifkin, Livingston, Levitan, and Silver; John Mercer, U.S. Senate staff; Dick Nathan, Rockefeller Institute; David Osborne, advisory board cochair of the Alliance for Redesigning Government; John Parr, Civic League; Bev Stein, Multnomah County chair; and Chris Wye, NAPA.

Alan Schrader, our editor at Jossey-Bass, worked through three rounds of draft manuscripts and, at critical points, put us on track to sharpen and focus the effort. Thanks are due as well to the editorial, marketing, and production staff at Jossey-Bass.

Other colleagues at the Alliance for Redesigning Government contributed in many key ways to this project. Gail Christopher, cochair, made all the right moves during the final stages of revising the book and guiding it into production. Neal Johnson, executive editor, and Ed Finkle, assistant editor, of *The Public Innovator* shared their stories and also provided an outlet for ours. And Nanette Rogers was always there to help us.

Finally, thanks are overdue to our partners, families, and many friends. This project, in tandem with so many others, has too often tried their patience. For their love and understanding we are forever grateful.

# The Authors

*Mark G. Popovich* is a senior partner and cofounder of The Public's Work, a Washington-based consulting group. Popovich provides research, project development, and technical assistance services to a variety of public and nonprofit organizations. Over his twenty-year career in the public and nonprofit sector, his work has focused on innovations in policy development and implementation at the state, local, and federal levels.

*Jack A. Brizius* (deceased) was a partner in the public policy consulting firm of Brizius and Foster and was president of U.S. Data on Demand, Inc. Prior to beginning his consulting work, he served in planning and policy positions in New Jersey, Illinois, and Pennsylvania state governments and was director of the Center for Policy Research at the National Governors' Association.

*Gail C. Christopher* is cochair and director of the Alliance for Redesigning Government and a fellow of the National Academy of Public Administration. She is author of *Peopling of America: Teacher's Guide and Manual* and developed the Americans All National Diversity Training program for educators and administrators. She is also author of *Anchors for the Innocent,* a popular trade book on parenting. She has, for the past twenty years, designed award-winning interventions that address major social policy concerns.

*Barbara R. Dyer* is a founding partner of The Public's Work. Prior to forming that national and international practice dedicated to improving government performance, Dyer cofounded and directed the National Academy of Public Administration's Alliance for Redesigning Government. Dyer is the author of several books, papers, and articles on public policy and management. She attended Clark University and the John F. Kennedy School of Government's Senior Executives in State and Local Government Program.

*Susan E. Foster* is vice president and director of Policy Research and Analysis at the National Center on Addiction and Substance Abuse at Columbia University. Prior to that, she was a partner in the public policy consulting firm of Brizius and Foster and was treasurer of U.S. Data on Demand, Inc. Foster has held policy and management positions in local, state, and federal governments and has provided consulting assistance to governments, corporations, and foundations on a broad range of public policy issues.

*Martha G. Miller* has taught organizational behavior at Yale and UCLA Management Schools. She has consulted to Fortune 500 companies and government organizations for twenty-five years on issues of diversity and high performance. Miller, an independent consultant in Washington, D.C., received her doctorate from Harvard University in 1980.

*Susan Resnick-West* is an Association for Quality and Participation Distinguished Faculty Member, an instructor for GOAL, QPC, and teaches in the Executive Development Program at the University of Southern California Graduate Business School. Among her clients are Xerox Corporation, Kaiser Permanente, Hughes Corporation, Harbor-UCLA Medical Center, Asian Development Bank, Ross Swiss Dairies, Kenneth Norris Jr. Cancer Hospital, ARCO, Chevron, Union Bank, P. L. Porter, and Pioneer LDCA.

*The Alliance for Redesigning Government,* part of the National Academy of Public Administration, is dedicated to improving government by linking the many thousands of people who are actively creating better ways to govern, learning from their efforts, and building better tools for change.

The National Academy of Public Administration is a nonprofit, nonpartisan, collegial organization chartered by Congress to improve governance at all levels—federal, state, and local. NAPA works toward that end chiefly by using the individual and collective experiences of its fellows to provide expert advice and counsel to government leaders. Its congressional charter, signed by President Reagan in 1984, was the first granted to a research organization since President Lincoln signed the charter for the National Academy of Sciences in 1863.

# Creating High-Performance
# Government Organizations

# ⟞⟋⟍⟞ Introduction: Welcome to the New World of Government

Welcome to the world of organizations that work. Are you a manager in government service? Are you an elected official? Are you a steward in a government employees' union? Or maybe you work in a nonprofit organization that delivers services under contract with a government agency. Are you dissatisfied with how your organization works—frustrated by the lack of clarity in its purpose, the complications of getting things done, or the inability to show results that really matter? Or are you part of a good organization but you see the potential to make it a great one? If you answered yes to any of these questions, this book was written for you.

Your dissatisfaction with how your organization works is undoubtedly related to the rapidly changing demands of the workplace. Organizations today are becoming artifacts of a time when life was more static. Yesterday, we rewarded stability and constancy, and our organizations served us well. Today, we value flexibility, adaptability, responsiveness, learning, and continuous improvement. Organizations do not change on their own. To meet new demands and challenges, we have to reinvent our organizations.

This process of reinvention involves helping people make a mental shift—a shift away from viewing organizations as static structures that may be renovated or rebuilt periodically and toward a model of organizations as growing, learning, and evolving systems. Organizational forms must become more flexible and able to adapt nimbly to a constantly changing environment. Even an agency that has behaved like a dinosaur for too many years to count can learn and change.

And change can be exciting. How does it feel to be part of a winning debate team, an accomplished musical ensemble, or a faith community that sustains its members? It feels great! We all get a charge from contributing to reaching important goals. By helping

1

your organization reach high performance, you and your colleagues can find that feeling where you work.

Creating high-performance organizations is not a linear process. It is a more organic process. It can start like a seed, sprouting anywhere in the organization. And it can grow where it finds open minds and nurturing attention. If you want to plant the seed or help an existing sprout of a new paradigm organization, you will need knowledge and tools.

## WHO CAN START THE CHANGE?

The decision to move to a high-performance organization can be made at virtually any level of the organization. You do not need to be the chief executive or an elected official to effectively initiate change. Obviously, you would have more power and resources to direct the change from a management position, but there is much that can be done by middle managers or front-line employees. Although the sphere of control is influenced by your position within a hierarchy, every person has the ability to improve performance within his or her own sphere of control.

In Iowa, for example, change started with a key part of the central management system and worked its way out into state government. It all began in the State Office of Administration (Rosenberg, 1994). The director of management was intrigued with a new way of budgeting—investment decision making—and began to explore its potential for the state. He convinced some colleagues to work with him and hired a consultant who had pioneered the concept. They held a work session for management and budgeting staff and specific agency personnel who either seemed responsive to the concept or who would have to be convinced of its value for it to work. From this modest, halting start, Iowa embarked on testing a new statewide process of investment decision making. Now, Iowa has a new state investment board and an extensive public involvement process.

Change began in San Jose, California, with individual pockets of creativity within city government (Finkle, 1995e). Eventually, these initiatives reached a critical mass and came to the attention of the city manager. Building on these initiatives, the city manager launched an organizational development strategy grounded in high-performance principles. First, the city's leadership sought to create a climate conducive to innovation across city government. They focused on customer service. Self-directed employee teams were a driving force in moving the process forward. Next, they focused on data-driven performance measurement for all departments and on improving process and cycle times. They implemented work simplification proposals from employees. A number of city departments and services were consolidated. And because the city believed that their customers would ultimately be the neighborhoods, the city created a neighborhood services department.

In other cases, elected officials harnessed their reach and authority to initiate change. In the federal government, for example, the National Performance Review (NPR) was begun because of the interest of Vice President Al Gore. In Oregon, the Multnomah County chair, Bev Stein, initiated a plan to transform county government. RESULTS (Reaching Excellent Service Using Leadership and Team Strategies) is aimed at empowering managers and employees so that they can provide quality service and practice continuous improvement. Above all, Multnomah County seeks to improve its ability to efficiently respond to the needs of its customers while improving the work life of employees.

Other examples of how the change process can start demonstrate the great diversity and potential that exists. Perhaps the only constant is that someone or some group begins the process because they are convinced of the need to change. Following are examples of how change can start.

• *Change from the middle.* Tired of the "silly regulations" that kept their agency from getting their customers into office space in a timely manner, the procurement staff of the Minneapolis Field Servicing Office decided to work smarter. Through their efforts, the office is maximizing the use of government discounts and saved half a million dollars in a single year for their Department of Agriculture customers. The team now completes 90 percent of its purchase orders within twenty-four hours. They boast an error rate of less than 1 percent. The office has become an effective competitor. The team now markets its services to other federal agencies as well.

• *Responding to market forces.* In Chester County, Pennsylvania, a school support agency (called an intermediate unit or IU) was threatened by the redirection of state funding away from the IUs to the local school districts (Finkle, 1995a). The IU director adapted the agency by developing an à la carte menu of educational and support services that create regional economies of scale. Agency officials identified areas in which they could offer comparative advantages to their customers, such as forming insurance consortiums and organizing bulk purchases of supplies. With the withdrawal of direct state funding, the IU could have withered away, but it did not. This IU is now competing with school districts to provide services.

• *Collaborating across sectors and between labor and management.* Ohio's Governor Voinovich initiated Quality Services Through Partnership—a program that is transforming state government into an organization in which employees work together to continuously improve how work is done. The change effort began with a public-private partnership between the state and Xerox. Xerox loaned an executive to adapt total quality management (TQM) training materials that had been proven effective in business to the needs of the public sector. Contrary to expectations, the union representing state employees was not a barrier. In fact, the union was Governor Voinovich's partner. The partnership includes equal numbers of labor and management leaders. Union and management employees, in fact, provide cotraining and cofacilitation throughout the departments.

• *Leadership from the legislative branch.* The push for boosting the performance of the federal government has also come from Congress. "The Government Performance and Results Act (GPRA), passed in 1993, is forcing a shift in federal agencies away from such traditional concerns as staffing and activity levels and toward a single overriding issue—results" (U.S. General Accounting Office, 1996, p. 1). Under GPRA, agencies are setting goals and improving measures of performance, and they are required to report on their accomplishments. GPRA is not a law Congress intends to "fire and forget" like a high-tech missile. Although responsibility for its implementation lies with federal managers throughout the agencies, Congress is seeking to maintain an active role in development and implementation.

As you can see from these examples, change can start anywhere in an organization. Once germinated, this change can even grow and cascade into large-scale reforms in the way organizations work. What is required is a commitment to change, a knowledge of the potential for change, and some understanding of what is involved in the change process itself. You already bring the first prerequisite to the task.

## SOURCES FOR THE IDEAS

We have drawn on case examples, literature reviews, professional experience, and field testing as the knowledge base for this book.

## Case Examples

We reviewed more than three dozen cases from a diverse group of public agencies at the local, state, and federal levels (Exhibit 1). At the midway point of our research, we also convened a select group of leading innovators from the federal level for a working seminar. The seminar allowed us to test ideas and garner more detailed insights from their examples.

The presenters and participants at that session included Bob Stone, staff director at the National Performance Review; Anna Goddard, director of the Employment and Training Administration's Reinvention Office; Carmen Maymi, NPR manager at the Bureau of Reclamation; Sue Fruchter, budget and strategic planning staff at the National Oceanic and Atmospheric Administration; and Steve Payne, national negotiator for Cooperative Efforts at the National Treasury Employees Union. Rigorous evaluations are seldom available for recent innovations. However, we did select cases for which the best information was available. In as many examples as possible, we have provided information on the results achieved in addition to describing key elements of the innovation.

## Literature Review

The project's first steps included months of work in reviewing articles, papers, books, and presentations. Sources tapped in the review varied from newspaper stories to professional journals. About seventy of these sources are cited; the References section provides the information necessary to help interested readers delve more deeply into some of the extensive literature in this field.

## Professional Experience

The experience of the seven members of the design team represents years of work in the public and private sectors. Each brings to the project lessons learned through careers involving the study, support, and implementation of innovations in a variety of organizational settings. Resnick-West and Miller have worked in the private sector as business consultants, as well as in academia. In combination, Brizius, Christopher, Dyer, Foster, and Popovich have worked with public sector leaders in all fifty state governments and on the federal and local levels. In addition, they have extensive management experience in the public and nonprofit sectors.

*Local*

Allegheny County, Pa.: Savings from Improving Child and Family Well-Being

Arlington, Va.: Principles of Government Service and Performance Improvement

Austin, Tex.: Public Health Clinic Process Redesign and Performance Improvement

Chester County, Pa.: Intermediate Unit, Education Support Agency

Chicago, Ill.: Neighborhood Improvement-Public Engagement, Agency Cooperation, and Performance Improvement

Cincinnati, Ohio: School District Peer Performance Review and Improvement

Hampton, Va.: Self-Managing Teams, Process Redesign, and Performance Improvement

Huron County, N.Y.: Bridge Replacement Cost-Cutting and Performance Improvement

Jacksonville, Fla.: Productivity Rewards for Employees

Multnomah County, Oreg.: Performance Measurement, Hiring, and Performance Assessments

New York, N.Y.: Probation Department Process Redesign and Performance Improvement

Phoenix, Ariz.: Public/Private Bidding for Performance Improvement in Waste Management

Richmond, Va.: Strategic Planning, Interagency Collaboration

San Jose, Calif.: Organizational Development Strategy

Sunnyvale, Calif.: Understanding and Changing Organizational Culture in the Public Sector

Tampa, Fla.: Assessing Customer Satisfaction and Performance Improvement

*State*

California: Value Effective Procurement

Hawaii: Office of Literacy Stakeholder Engagement, Planning, and Performance Improvement

Hawaii: Alternative Approaches for Negotiating Labor Contracts

Iowa: Investment Budgeting and Performance Management

Maryland: Welfare Reform Planning and Performance Improvement

Michigan: Comprehensive Procurement Reforms

Minnesota: Minnesota Milestones, Benchmarking, and Performance Measurement

Minnesota: Procurement Performance Improvements

Ohio: Strategic Planning and Stakeholder Engagement for Improving Services for Children and Families

Ohio: Quality Services Through Partnership

Oregon: Strategic Planning, Performance Measurement, Building Accountability

Oregon: Computer-Based Vendor Information Program

Tennessee: Strategic Planning and Visioning for Improving Literacy, Texas Literacy Improvement and Performance Management Systems

Washington: Washington Management Service Civil Service Reforms and Procurement Reforms

Wisconsin: Improvements in Procurement of Information Technology

**Exhibit 1.    Listing of Cases and Examples.**

*Federal*

Bureau of Reclamation: Performance Improvement

Defense Personnel Support Center: Improvements in Procurement

Department of Agriculture: Alternative Hiring Strategies

Department of Agriculture: Procurement Service Improvement

Federal Aviation Administration: Performance Improvement and Procurement
Reforms

Federal Emergency Management Agency: Strategic Planning, Process Redesign, and
Developing Partnerships

National Oceanic and Atmospheric Administration: Planning and Performance
Budgeting

National Performance Review: Government-wide Performance Improvement

Veterans Health Administration: Performance Measurement and Improvement

Exhibit 1.    Listing of Cases and Examples *(continued)*.

## Field Testing

At regular intervals throughout the project, our drafts were refined by
the ultimate test: Did our ideas and viewpoints comport with the real-
world experience of front-line innovators? The working group and reviewers (listed in the Acknowledgments section) were very active in
shaping the development of the book. The writing team also presented
materials from the project at meetings and seminars at which the material could be critiqued and the team could find additional case examples. These presentations included the Annual Conference of the
Florida Association of Public Purchasing Officials, the Annual Meeting of the Delaware Association of Nonprofit Agencies, the National
Association of Public Administration's Human Resources Consor-
tium, and the New York State Quality Through Participation Seminar.

Finally, some writing team members worked on a more sustained
basis with three groups to test ideas and develop material for the book.
Throughout the last three years, Mark Popovich and Barbara Dyer
worked with the federal, state, and local partners of the Oregon Option. The Option is building from the state's experience in performance benchmarking to develop a more effective and flexible
intergovernmental partnership. Working with the city manager, top
agency officials, and the city council in Richmond in 1995 and 1996,
allowed the project to help support and learn from that city's efforts
at strategic planning and performance improvement. And over the
past year, we have learned from and supported strategic planning, goal
setting, and systems reform efforts at the Maryland Department of
Human Resources.

## OVERVIEW OF THE BOOK

Those of you reading this book probably come from very different organizations and from different levels within those organizations. Consequently, you will have different perspectives on and knowledge about the new, emerging high-performance work organizations.

Differences in background and vantage point should not be a problem in using the material, however. The book offers examples or models from both the private and public sectors and from all levels of government—models and experiences that reflect change efforts beginning at quite different places within organizations and in quite different ways. The book does not provide one model. Rather, it offers information and tools that you can use to help build your own organizations that work.

This book is designed to help you develop high-performance organizations in government. We consider the book's content to be an evolving product that will be enriched by the experience of those of you creating your own high-performance organizations. Accordingly, the Alliance invites you to contribute your experience to this knowledge base.

You can contact the Alliance for Redesigning Government at the National Academy of Public Administration, 1120 G Street, N.W., Suite 850, Washington, DC 20005, (202) 347–3190.

This book has three main sections. Part One (Chapters One, Two, and Three) provides background information on the context in which these changes are taking place, including a discussion of the political considerations in making the transition to high performance in government.

Part Two (Chapters Four through Seven) is a guide to the key steps in the change process. You will also find tools to help you along the way.

Part Three (Chapters Eight through Eleven) suggests a wide range of approaches you can use to reform outdated central management systems in order to support high performance throughout your organization.

We strongly suggest that you explore the complete volume before instituting any change in your organization. Although the process of change itself is not linear, the chapters are linked and build on each other. Within each chapter, you will find some references to other sections. These references will help you use the book to explore ideas and tools that will work for you in your own unique setting. Taken as a whole, they give you a much richer understanding of how to create organizations that work than you would get from exploring just one or two chapters that seem to address your immediate concern.

# PART ONE

# Meeting the Challenges of Improving Government Performance

# CHAPTER ONE

# Understanding High-Performance Organizations

There is much confusion in the public sector about just what is meant by *high-performance organization.* Terms like *total quality management, reengineering,* and *reinvention* are bandied about sometimes, leaving managers and employees more confused than enlightened.

All of these terms, and others like them, refer to approaches to improving the performance of organizations. All are aimed at equipping organizations and the people in them to work better and to be more efficient and responsive to change.

If that is your direction, you will need a working definition of high-performance organizations. *High-performance organizations are groups of employees who produce desired goods or services at higher quality with the same or fewer resources. Their productivity and quality improve continuously, from day to day, week to week, and year to year, leading to the achievement of their mission.*

Several points about this definition deserve a closer look. First, the process of transformation and of maintaining the change is people-centered in high-performance organizations. We are not simply talking about processes, technologies, or techniques. These are important, but the essential focus is on the people inside the organizations and those on the outside with a vested interest in its performance. The processes, technologies, and techniques are tools to help them perform at a higher level.

Second, a high-performance organization may or may not encompass the entire organization or organizational unit. The definition refers to groups of employees, regardless of the extent of their span of control. Change can start in pockets within organizations and cascade to a systemwide initiative. Eventually, for an entire organization to be high performing, all its components must be involved, including its central management systems. Top leaders in our organizations need not be the initiators of the move to high performance, but eventually their permission, if not encouragement, is needed for change to permeate the organization.

Third, high-performance organizations are not restricted to traditional organizational boundaries. They can encompass different bureaus and agencies. They even create links across levels of government and across the boundaries of the public and private sectors. A hallmark of high-performance organizations is the blurring of rigid lines that hinder the collaboration and change that can yield better results. The focus of the people in such organizations shifts from traditional boundaries to the results they are trying to achieve.

Fourth, the term *desired goods and services* in the definition refers to things that make the greatest contribution to achieving the mission. High-performance organizations focus on their mission. Some police departments, for example, are judged based on changes in the number of arrests. But if the number of criminals collared is sharply up, has the safety of citizens and their property improved? If improved public safety is the goal, arrests are, at best, an imperfect guide. Changes in rates of violent crime would be a better yardstick. Measures of whether people in neighborhoods feel safer might be better still. As a high-performance organization hones its mission, it changes what it does and how it does it. The point is to get the results that really matter.

Fifth, high-performance organizations produce their results using the same or fewer resources. They are competitive and sensitive to bottom-line pressure. They use crisis in government—declining resources, for example—as an opportunity for working smarter and producing better.

Finally, high-performance organizations are dynamic, continually evolving entities. People in these organizations are undergoing the same processes of dynamic involvement and continual growth. The organizational model for a high-performance organization is a biological one. Organizations are, in a sense, alive. They grow and change in response to their own needs and those of the environment. Accordingly, these new types of organizations have characteristics, like organizing genes, that distinguish them from more traditional organizations.

Before we discuss more fully the characteristics of high-performance organizations, we need to think about just why organizations should strive to become more high performing. What are the pressures you feel as a manager, an elected official, a labor leader, or an employee to change the way your organization works? Why are public sector organizations moving in this direction?

## WHY DEVELOP HIGH-PERFORMANCE ORGANIZATIONS IN GOVERNMENT?

In recent years, the public has witnessed the successful transition in many private companies to more results-based management. We see many organizations that do more with less. As consumers, we demand that organizations focus on both the value and quality of their products or services.

What we demand of businesses—value, quality, innovation, customer service—we also want from the public sector. In response, there are efforts being made across federal and state agencies and a much more broad-based movement within local government to meet and exceed these expectations. The public demands it. And in the public sector, we owe it to them.

Fiscal pressures and voter demands for better performance are motivating change as well. A growing number of people in government are determined to change systems and incentives so that dedicated employees are encouraged to improve productivity and quality in whatever they do.

Other trends, such as a changing workforce and technological improvements, also converge to make change both necessary and possible. These changes are part of a broader reshaping of our attitudes toward work and our organizations. For government officials at all levels, union leaders, and other innovators, it is important to understand why government should make this sometimes painful transition to a new form of management and operation.

# IDENTIFYING FORCES OF CHANGE

A discussion of the major factors in creating a need for change follows.

## Fiscal Pressures

Fiscal pressures result because government budgets seem perpetually tight. Demands for services always seem to outstrip available revenues. Those who want government to do more recognize that it must do what it does now—but do it better. Those who would shrink government's role want high performance as well. Everybody wants government to sharpen its focus on producing results that matter for people and their families. Regardless of the fiscal posture of a political leader, fiscal pressures demand better performance from government.

## Sophisticated and Demanding Consumers

Consumers are another force for change. They expect more and demand more. We all see the myriad benefits of the ongoing revolutions in quality, service, and productivity constantly in our daily lives. New services are offered through information technology and many other innovations.

For example, with a network of automatic teller machines, you can do your banking when and where you need to. You need not go to a bank during regular banking hours. You may be at home; it may be late; or maybe you need cash to pay your restaurant check during a tour of Italy. Another example is the use of electronic mail. Air mail was fine in its day. Now, we send electronic mail through the Internet when next-day delivery seems too slow. Also, customers demand products and services that offer money-back guarantees. We are increasingly living in a world where goods can be produced, information exchanged, and services provided in a very short time. It should not be a surprise that consumers demand the same level of service from government.

## Changing Workforce

The changing workforce creates pressure. Within both government and the private sector, the labor force is changing dramatically. High-performance organizations demand highly skilled workers, even as demographic changes and the limitations of our current education system limit the supply. Government competes with the private sector for the best workers—competition that will only become more fierce. And the public sector will too often lose out if it does not provide job satisfaction and more freedom to produce. In addition, unions representing government workers, along with the workers themselves, are demanding more meaningful and satisfying work. To get job satisfaction, workers must participate in more effective organizations—organizations that get results.

## Perceptions of Waste and Inefficiency

Perceptions of waste and inefficiency are also influential. Government has succeeded in solving or significantly reducing many problems in our nation, states, and localities. At the same time, most citizens believe that government is inefficient and ineffective in providing what they value most: personal security, education, jobs, and opportunities for the future. As public cynicism has deepened, the impetus for all levels of government to improve productivity and quality grows ever stronger. If the public believes government overpromises and underdelivers, government can change attitudes and win support by improving its performance.

## New Technologies

New technologies create new opportunities. The explosion of information technologies has altered the way America works. Over thirty-five million Americans now have home offices. Nearly instant communication helps the smallest businesses compete globally. Advances in biotechnology, medicine, materials, and many other areas are altering the shape of the world economy and the global workforce.

These same technologies are or can be available to government agencies. With them, government agencies can have greater freedom to organize more flexibly and serve customers more effectively. In the public sector, many unions are advocates of technology in the workplace. They see that technology is needed to get the public's work done. And when it is done right, it can also improve the working lives of its members.

New technologies are also giving consumers the ability to abandon public sector services for better-performing options. The advent of technologies that force competition with traditional public sector services put pressure on government to improve performance.

As the private sector improves quality and productivity, government leaders watch with a combination of admiration and skepticism. Can the techniques employed by businesses help improve productivity and quality in government? Will these improvements be visible enough to counteract the growing cynicism of voters and taxpayers? Are these techniques fads? Or are they real tools that are applicable in the public sector? Many government leaders and workers are already adapting them and demonstrating that these techniques can yield impressive improvements. They can be effective and sustainable, and they can yield results that matter.

To move toward high performance, we must have a better idea of just what the goal is. What does a high-performance organization look like? How does it differ from what we have today? If you are a champion of change in your organization, the first tool in your kit should be a clear understanding of the characteristics of high-performance organizations.

## CHARACTERISTICS OF HIGH-PERFORMANCE ORGANIZATIONS

By looking at many different strategies for helping organizations become more effective, efficient, and adaptable, common characteristics and themes emerge. By examining closely the characteristics that make both qualitative and quantitative differences in high-performance organizations, we can distill the essential differences (see Exhibit 1.1).

---

High-performance organizations . . .

- Are clear on their mission
- Define outcomes and focus on results
- Empower employees
- Motivate and inspire people to succeed
- Are flexible and adjust nimbly to new conditions
- Are competitive in terms of performance
- Restructure work processes to meet customer needs
- Maintain communications with stakeholders

---

Exhibit 1.1.    Principles of High-Performance Organizations.

*High-performance organizations are clear about their mission.* Advocates of high-performance workplaces are moving toward a mission mentality and away from a primary focus on programs. Their missions are often defined through a broad-based process involving those with an interest in the outcome of the organization. The mission statement and the process for developing it bring into focus a compelling picture of the future toward which the organization is moving. This clarity of mission sets the framework for assessing the performance of the organization.

For example, the Federal Bureau of Reclamation recognized that changing external conditions necessitated a fundamental change in the agency's mission (Maymi, 1995). Bureau dams generated power and delivered the water necessary to support settlement, economic growth, and recreation across the arid West. But growth of demand for water continues to outstrip the resource base. And few underdeveloped sites remain for water control systems. The bureau's job from its inception—construction and project management—must change. This involves transforming itself from a civil engineering and construction agency to a world leader in water resource management. The bureau adopted this change without a change in federal legislation.

The first step taken in shifting the agency mission was to form a group of employees, primarily from field offices. They met, without senior executive service or management representation, to develop a blueprint for change. To tap the ideas of all employees, the bureau kept all meetings and documents open to organized labor. The group's report was distributed to all six thousand employees, who were encouraged to review and comment. Town hall meetings, small-group work sessions, and on-line discussions with the agency director were all used to get input from across the far-flung agency on the report's recommendations. When it was settled, managers were challenged with developing a plan and implementing the changes.

*High-performance organizations define outcomes and focus on results.* Starting from this vision or mission statement, high-performance organizations define specific outcomes that they will achieve to accomplish their mission. Defining these outcomes requires the involvement of the stakeholders. Measures of performance are developed and communicated in a timely way to the entire workforce. Outcomes and performance measures are tools the organization and its stakeholders use to focus on results.

The federal Veterans Health Administration (VHA) is using a tool that is as effective as the sharpest scalpel to improve medical services for veterans. By revamping its data analysis efforts, the VHA is getting detailed information on medical outcomes. The agency is using this performance information to better safeguard the health and lives of veterans. For example, by tracking the success of heart surgeries at VHA facilities, they identified differences in surgical outcomes among forty-three centers performing cardiac surgeries. After analyzing the data, VHA recommended techniques and processes for shortening postoperative hospital stays and cutting the risks of infections or complications. Because the VHA adopted these and other techniques, cardiac teams lowered their mortality rates over the last eight years by an average of 13 percent (U.S. General Accounting Office, 1996).

*High-performance organizations empower their employees.* Employees are the vital core of a high-performance organization. To reach high performance, employees are empowered to apply their skills, creativity, ability to adapt to change, and capacity to be continuous learners to achieve the organization's mission. Employees are empowered to form alliances and working relationships based on their interest in meeting the outcomes and mission of the organization. They are not limited by organizational boundaries.

How well employees rise to the challenge of applying their skills to fulfilling the mission of the organization, develop new skills, and dedicate themselves to continuous learning will, in large part, determine the success of the organization.

Cincinnati teachers helped hold down costs and improve education by using a peer performance review process they developed. In this process, administrators and teachers evaluate new hires and some veterans. They set high standards for new hires. And after the first year, their dismissal rates went up. More veteran teachers are also referred for intervention. The new system includes clear career ladders. Lead teachers are designated to assume additional responsibilities and are reimbursed with an additional stipend of $5,000 per year. The results of these and other steps are impressive indeed. Over two years, the number of administrators was halved. And the teachers and their new system helped the school board realize the first balanced budget in seven years (Finkle, 1995c).

*High-performance organizations institute new processes to motivate and inspire people to succeed.* In high-performance organizations, employees are encouraged to collaborate and develop new and decentralized approaches to achieving the desired outcomes. They develop and reengineer new processes for completing tasks, including rethinking the tasks themselves in light of the organization's overall mission. There are incentives to form alliances for a pragmatic reason—to achieve results. Alliances span work groups, departments, agencies, and operating levels. They even cross boundaries between the public and private sectors. The rules governing these alliances are flexible and consistent with achieving better outcomes for the customers.

When the New York City Probation Department faced a $3.3 million budget cut over four years, losing one-third of its officers, it changed the way it did business. Refocused on reducing recidivism, they determined to pay more attention to violent and younger offenders (Finkle, 1995d). At the same time, the department instituted a process of "virtual probation," in which thirty thousand, lower-risk probationers now report to the probation office via kiosks placed throughout the city. Lower-risk probationers are analyzed based on the offender's age, prior record, and other important factors. As appropriate, probationers are steered to group sessions, kiosks, or mid-level supervision. The department asked its employees to do a better job with fewer resources. Incentives for workers included sharing in the productivity savings, and the workload is better managed by cutting the number of intensive cases assigned to each worker.

*High-performance organizations are flexible, adaptable, and quick to adjust when conditions change.* People in high-performance organizations understand the mission of the organization and collaborate to institute new processes when necessary. Managers recruit people with broad, transferable skills. Workers are encouraged to initiate, innovate, and take risks. They are promoted based on objective measures of performance, and both managers and labor are committed to training and continuous improvement.

New York's Huron County faced the prospect of repairing or replacing two hundred crumbling bridges at a price it could not afford to pay. But the county found a way to both accelerate bridge replacements and cut costs. It was not magic. It did take equal parts of common sense, careful analysis, and sharp dealing. Private contractors, they found, would take too long and cost too much. They proved the public sector could do it better, faster, and cheaper. The workforce to do the job was already on the county payroll. Employees were redeployed from seasonal work; they were trained and then reassigned to bridge repair. The costs of equipment rental and supplies were put under the microscope. As it turned out, it cost $1,000 to rent a crane for each bridge, and buying a new crane cost only $15,000. Steel was purchased at a savings of 10 cents per pound by bulk buying. In just two years, this team of public employees replaced or repaired twenty-five bridges—more than three times the number of bridges that contractors would have done. And their average cost per bridge was 40 percent lower.

*High-performance organizations are competitive in terms of performance.* High-performance workplaces are clear about their bottom line. They know what their mission is and what policy and program outcomes they must achieve to accomplish their mission. This knowledge provides an opportunity for competition against their own record, as well as against other organizations. High-performance organizations are characterized by collaborative and cooperative working relationships within the organization. The performance of the organization itself, however, is highly competitive with other, similarly focused organizations or with past performance.

The business-oriented leaders of Phoenix, for example, demand that public services be provided at highest quality and least cost. They believe that whoever can do the job best—a public agency or a private company—should get the job. Phoenix uses public bidding between city departments and private contractors to get the best value for taxpayers. Waste management is a prime example. The city put a contract out for bid for bulk garbage collection in one of its districts. In the first round, the Department of Public Works (DPW) bid but lost to a private contractor. In fact, DPW lost four years in a row. Then the employees began to do what private sector businesses do. To improve performance, drivers redesigned the routes and the jobs. Trucks and routes were assigned to designated drivers to cut repair costs. They worked together to improve the effectiveness and cut the costs of equipment maintenance. As improved technology became available, DPW bought it. Labor and management worked together to improve the working environment and provide the training. Bonuses and other awards were offered. And they implemented a plan to extend the life of the landfill. The bid losers became winners once again. In the fifth competition, DPW offered the winning bid. They were the best in the sixth and seventh rounds as well.

*High-performance organizations restructure their work processes to meet customer needs.* High performance means meeting customers' needs. High-performance organizations emphasize quality, value, customer satisfaction, and results rather than compliance with rules and regulations. They start from the premise that customer engagement leads to higher quality and greater customer satisfaction. They are committed to reaching out and involving customers in the process of quality improvement.

Front-line caseworkers in the public health clinics in Austin, Texas, took the lead in restructuring services to better meet customer needs (Barnett, 1994). They began with an ambitious goal—get patients in, served, and out in one hour. To reach that goal, they redesigned the system. Rather than shuttling about, patients stay in one place. Clinic workers rotate. Color-coded flags steer clinic employees to provide patients with just-in-time service. Any step that does not require the patient's presence is deferred until after the visit. The clinic cut back on forms. They increased the number of copiers. Appointment, scheduling, and discharge procedures were revamped. As a result, Austin is paying less for more. The clinic cut costs by 12 percent while increasing the number of clinic visits by 14 percent. These changes have brought commitment throughout the clinics on the part of staff because they are providing services more efficiently and better meeting customer needs. Are the patients happy? Prior to these changes, only 8 percent of patients were in and out within an hour. Now, 82 percent meet this standard.

*High-performance organizations maintain open and productive communications among stakeholders.* Successful organizations develop effective channels of communication to keep stakeholders involved in the process of continuous improvement. Effective communications provide information on progress toward achievement of desirable outcomes and the mission. In addition, open communication allows new ideas to surface. It allows customer perceptions and suggestions to be absorbed and acted upon. And mission and outcomes can continually be reevaluated. Communications systems in high-performance organizations work effectively for managers, staff, unions, appointed and elected leaders, customers, and other stakeholders.

Chicago Mayor Richard M. Daley's Strategic Neighborhood Action Project (SNAP) brings public agencies together at the community level to hear what communities need and deliver the services they want (Popovich, 1995). Neighborhoods compete for participation. The community puts together an action plan that demonstrates neighborhood leadership and commitment. At the neighborhood level, as one participant remarked, coordination of public agencies has been viewed as an "unnatural act between very nonconsenting partners." Now, four city departments must cooperate to expedite services, co-ordinate work schedules, and equip programs. The result is one-stop access to services with a single point of contact for all agencies. That eases communication between public agencies and the neighborhood. And time and costs are saved by delivering services more efficiently.

## DESIGN COMPONENTS OF HIGH-PERFORMANCE ORGANIZATIONS

The design of high-performance organizations also differs from more traditional enterprises. For example, what is the difference in the skills of the people, the information and decision-making systems, the human resource systems, the structure, leadership style, and even the culture, in the two types of organizations (see Exhibit 1.2)?

| Design Components | Traditional Organizations | High-Performance Organizations |
| --- | --- | --- |
| People | Narrow expertise<br>Rugged individuals | Multiskilled<br>Team players |
| Decision Systems | Centralized<br>Closed | Dispersed<br>Open |
| Human Resource Systems | Standardized selection<br>Routine training<br>Job-based pay<br>Narrow, repetitive jobs | Realistic job interviews<br>Continuous training<br>Performance-based pay<br>Enriched jobs<br>Self-regulating teams |
| Structure | Tall, rigid hierarchies<br>Functional departments | Flat, flexible hierarchies<br>Self-contained businesses |
| Values and Culture | Promote compliance<br>Routine behaviors | Promote involvement,<br>innovation, and cooperation |

**Exhibit 1.2.    Comparison of Traditional and High-Performance Organizations.**

*Source*: Resnick-West, 1994, p. 34.

# CHAPTER TWO

# Challenges and Opportunities for Change in the Public Sector

F ederal, state, and local governments have experienced many waves of reform in the twentieth century. Line item budgeting, the civil service, management by objectives, competitive bidding, and many other practices were innovative improvements at the time they were implemented. They often arose from a crisis. Or they reflected a growing body of knowledge about the management sciences for large organizations. Particularly in their application, they both reflected and influenced the shape and culture of our organizations.

As we approach the dawn of a new millennium, the needs of our public agencies are mutating, and they will continue to change at a rapid pace. As public servants, we confront challenging and exciting times. Progress may entail constant struggle, but the only option we cannot take is to stand still.

In the quest for high performance, many of the practices and systems developed as reforms in the past will demand refinement. Others can only be abandoned and replaced. As in other organizations, the processes of government evolve and require continuous change and improvement to keep up with rising expectations, technological innovations, and changing demands.

Your movement toward high performance can be guided by a systemwide perspective. Or, given the challenges, tools, and authority available to you, your strategy may be to create pockets of innovative practices within a larger, more traditional organization.

Either approach can yield important gains. Experience in the private and public sectors, however, strongly suggests that reaching high-performance potential entails a systemwide commitment. Virtually an entire organization must change to achieve the highest possible levels of productivity and quality.

Fortunately, systemic change can start at many different places in an organization and can spread throughout the organization with positive results. Innovations by even a small cluster of change agents can spark broader involvement in other parts of the larger organization. In this way, pilots provide the most concrete illustration of how the larger organization should evolve toward high performance.

Regardless of your initial strategy choice—a systemwide approach or an approach through pockets of innovation—high-performance organizations must be developed in manageable steps. Over time, all facets of the organization and its basic systems will be affected.

Before discussing what "manageable steps" might look like, it is important to understand the nature of the changes that must occur for organizations to shift to high-performance models. The characteristics of high-performance organizations described in Chapter One provide helpful background. Realizing the underlying types of change that make it possible for these characteristics to emerge within an organization is essential.

## TYPES OF CHANGE IN SHIFTING
## TO HIGH-PERFORMANCE MODELS

The characteristics that distinguish high-performance organizations from others involve three basic categories of change. These are

- Change in the relationship between people and their work
- Change in the relationship between organizations and their customers
- Change in the relationship between organizations and their external environment

## Change Between People and Their Work

Henry Ford did not invent the assembly line or mass production, but he did perfect them (Lacey, 1986). In so doing, he built a company and launched another economic revolution. Ford Motor Company, as a highly tuned manufacturing machine, was a marvel in its age. Henry Ford's methods and the organizational cultures that supported them were quickly adapted in manufacturing and other sectors. Successful ideas are contagious. And as the size and complexity of the public sector grew, government also caught the bug.

About one hundred years have come and gone. But if you step back to take a long view of how our agencies organize and structure work, you will undoubtedly see the echoes of Henry Ford's ideas. Tasks are often broken down into small parts and parceled out in an assembly-line style.

The welfare intake worker, for example, knows what to ask and how to ask it in order to complete the forms. The forms are passed to supervisors, who review them with an eye to limiting the agency's error rates. As the forms stack up, they are transferred to another specialist for eligibility determination. The decision gets passed to the caseworker. The caseworker informs the applicant. Data processing is told to issue the benefit check.

For many years and many agencies, this approach to organizing tasks worked rather well. But organizing work in this way also can exact a heavy price. When all you see is your small piece of the overall task, where is the incentive to innovate or even to coordinate across tasks? What part of such a system is accountable for either great success or miserable failure?

Many businesses learned a hard lesson in the eighties and nineties. When tasks are atomized to minute, individual elements, people too often perform them mechanically. They have little concern for the relationship of their work to that of other parts of the organization. Productivity and quality often slump.

Routine may be easy to teach and to learn. It may be easier still to monitor. But it can stifle creativity and hinder employees (and the organizations they work in) from realizing their full potential.

In high-performance organizations, the relationship between people and their work changes. Employees are challenged to relate their tasks or activities to the overall outcome to be achieved. Work processes, structures, procedures, and even the tasks themselves are changed as needed to better achieve the outcome.

For example, the city of Hampton, Virginia, is changing the nature of work by experimenting with self-managing teams. The Human Resources Department (HRD) started first. To make it work, HR employees were cross-trained to broaden and deepen their skills. Rigid procedures and assignments were abandoned. The teams manage the work. Each week they take the agency's in-basket and decide who will do what. The city's Parks and Recreation Department started a little later. Parks employees flattened the agency hierarchy and formed teams that are organized into geographic divisions. Did the transformation come easily? Did it go smoothly? Not always. According to one manager, "At first employees were somewhat catatonic over the magnitude of the change." But Hampton also found that preparation paid off. "In order to make this change, we first had to build a lot of trust." As the new approach has unfolded, Hampton is improving efficiency and effectiveness and adapting better to new challenges. Worker morale is definitely up.

## Change Between Organizations and Their Customers

How many times this month have you been in a meeting where the agency was "us" and customers and other stakeholders were "them"? In many of these cases, employees are showing allegiance to their organization. But too often it comes at the expense of the customers.

High-performance organizations work hard to break down this us-them dichotomy. Meeting customer needs means success to them. They find creative ways to involve customers in helping them achieve their mission. If change is needed to accommodate customer needs, everything is on the table. It may take employee training or tossing out outmoded procedures. Work may be reorganized, or the bureaucracy may be sharply pruned. It may not be easy to do. But to meet customer needs, it gets done.

When a natural disaster strikes, it is the job of the Federal Emergency Management Agency (FEMA) to coordinate federal help. But too often, FEMA was not ready to meet the real needs of victims and their communities when the call came in. To better meet those needs, the agency completed its first-ever strategic planning effort and a major reorganization in 1993 (U.S. General Accounting Office, 1996). Preparing in advance of disasters meant building partnerships with other local, state, and federal organizations. For example, Hurricane Andrew devastated homes and businesses in South Florida in 1992. Since then, FEMA has been working with the housing industry and local governments to improve building codes. Particularly when it comes to disasters, prevention is often better and less costly than treatment after the fact.

## Change Between Organizations and Their External Environment

Traditional organizations often gird their loins to protect themselves from the outside world. Their boundaries are sharply drawn and unyielding. In high-performance organizations, elements of the external environment are viewed as potential resources or allies in achieving the agency's mission. Boundaries are intentionally blurred, and the focus shifts from maintaining the boundary to achieving the mission.

The future presents few opportunities for adults who have limited literacy skills. Hawaii was investing in programs to help them, but the Office of Literacy and Lifelong Learning (OLLL) was frustrated that their efforts weren't making greater progress. Rather than simply looking inward for answers, the OLLL enlisted stakeholders from inside and outside government. The list was intentionally a long one. It included other state and local agencies, customers, foundations, nonprofits, corporations, service providers, legislators, university representatives, and a local think-tank. This broad-based development group set off on a unique process of organizational reform. After much research, they decided to develop a performance-based system of providing services. A common vision was developed. They set goals and performance measures and designed a measurement and reporting system. They also drew up plans for full implementation and for ensuring that the new approach would support continuous improvement goals. And perhaps most important, by working together they changed the relationship between those in government and the outside environment. On their own, the OLLL can make a dent in ending illiteracy. With their allies, they can reach a new level of results that really matter to the people they want to help.

Understanding the types of change necessary for high performance provides a footing for beginning to build your own change efforts. Before you proceed, however, you should also review some of the major challenges you will face.

## CHALLENGES IN MOVING TO HIGH PERFORMANCE

The evolution toward high-performance work organizations began in the private sector. As the public sector adapted the techniques of high-performing private sector organizations for its own use, challenges emerged that reflect the differences between private and public organizations.

People apply different labels and package design changes and tools for change in different ways. The process of moving from a bureaucratic to a high-performing organization is called, for example, *reinvention, redesign,* or *transformation.* Examples of specific tools employed are *total quality management* (TQM), *process reengineering,* or *self-managing work teams.* The finished product is referred to as a *high-performance organization* or, alternatively, a *learning organization.*

This proliferation of terms can confuse those in the public sector who are attempting to apply the knowledge gained to their own efforts. Regardless of the label, the important point is that behind these labels is the list of characteristics just described. The emphasis and inspirational appeal may vary with the approach, but their similarities are more important than their differences.

The task facing the public sector is not to simply lift, for example, the TQM tool and drop it into government. Nor are self-managing work teams a quick fix. Many of those in government have already witnessed ill-fated examples of people struggling to use tools such as these without a larger understanding of why and for what purpose they are doing it. Rather, the task is to inculcate the underlying characteristics of high-performance organizations and to carefully tailor them to your organization's unique challenges and opportunities.

As you work to adapt the organization to these characteristics, some important challenges will arise:

- The challenge of structure
- The challenge of measuring performance

• The challenge of identifying customers
• The challenge of supporting intrapreneurship
• The challenge of continuous learning

## The Challenge of Structure

How many times have you heard someone assert that government must become more like private sector businesses? Although it has become standard fare on the campaign trail, advocates of this position are only partly right; many public sector agencies do not face some important problems found frequently in businesses.

Decision-making authority, for example, is more dispersed in the public sector. Centralization never fully took hold in a politicized environment. Compared to many large corporations, the hierarchies of government are not as tall. In addition, many team-oriented nuclei are already operating in service agencies. And information systems are often dispersed, if not open.

But dispersed authority presents other challenges, such as the blurring of the lines between the roles of legislative and executive branches. For the past thirty years, legislatures and city councils built their independent capacities to formulate budgets, set priorities, and conduct close oversight of executive agencies.

In some states and localities, however, legislative bodies have slipped beyond these important functions to take on a micromanagement approach to running government. Micromanagement by legislative bodies can dampen performance by public agencies. In some cases, it creates a culture in which too much focus is placed on eliminating any possible mistakes and not enough attention is paid to innovation. Managers are not given the authority, resources, or incentives to manage.

In these cases, reorienting legislative bodies to focus on outcomes and results rather than micromanagement is a challenge for administrators and legislators alike.

This challenge might be met by negotiating on a vision and sorting and realigning roles. Legislative bodies should play a central role in thinking strategically about what their level of government should or should not be doing. They are well positioned to help define mission and goals. And they should develop an accountability system, including regular oversight, to make sure public resources are used effectively to meet public goals.

There are also problems of structure within the executive branch itself. Achieving high performance in public agencies will necessitate reforming central management systems such as planning, budgeting, personnel, information management, and purchasing. These systems must be flexible enough to support innovation at the agency level. Those who have government high-performance workplace initiatives under way advise a stronger focus on preventing central management processes from stifling reform efforts by imposing rigid controls on hiring, purchasing, budgeting, and planning. (Chapters Eight through Eleven discuss approaches to reforming central management systems to support high performance.)

## The Challenge of Measuring Performance

A second challenge in government involves the lack of performance measurement systems. These systems enable us to track how well and how timely our efforts are progressing toward achieving our vision.

Private businesses have many performance measures (quantifiable or qualitative tools to assess whether policies or programs are contributing to the achievement of a desirable policy or program outcome or result). They can rely on these indicators to measure whether new approaches are working.

Government needs to put better performance measurement systems in place. To do this, government must first be clear on its overall vision and the results it expects to achieve. This will not be easy. It will take time and resources, and it will test the patience of front-line service providers and top managers alike. But the value of good performance measurement systems far outweighs the difficulties likely to be encountered in building them. (See Chapter Seven.)

## The Challenge of Identifying Customers

Another principle of high-performance organizations is to keep a tight focus on what the customer wants, shedding any and all functions that do not lead directly to customer satisfaction. This poses particular problems for government because it is often difficult to define just who the customer is. Is the customer the service recipient, the lawmaker, the financier, or the general public?

Customers may be defined one way in the case of motor vehicle registration services but another way in the case of law enforcement.

Or we may have to realize that, in many cases, government has multiple customers whose needs must be balanced.

Even when the customer is clearly identified, public agencies often have little information about what the customer actually wants. Even when the customers are defined well, governments often try to give them what they think the customers need rather than what they want.

Without market signals, public agencies must find other methods for judging customer satisfaction. A high-performance agency must define its customers very clearly, find out what they want, and focus laser-like attention on providing value to those customers. Public agencies can do this successfully. However, no government in this country has implemented as radical a program as many restructured corporations have, because to do so could cause enormous levels of disruption, layoffs, and fundamental shifts in political power.

## The Challenge of Supporting Intrapreneurship

High-performance organizations emphasize employee ingenuity and intrapreneurship within a larger structure. *Intrapreneurship* can be defined as organizing and managing a new and creative enterprise inside government.

Intrapreneurship is often difficult to sustain without an organizationwide commitment. This can be particularly challenging when the culture of the larger organization is averse to change or risk. Existing incentives to employees are to stay within their traditional organizational boundaries.

To reach high performance, agencies need to create an environment in which intrapreneurship can flourish. Supporting self-designing and self-managing work teams is one approach. Innovations spawned by intrapreneurs will not reform an organization overnight, but they can be a significant way to build positive experience in moving toward high performance. Nothing succeeds—and invites replication—like proven success.

Self-designing work organizations require a decentralized governance structure and plenty of flexibility and tolerance for changes in procedures—with a concomitant emphasis on performance—from central management systems. In addition, methods of measuring results must be in place to determine whether various self-designed work processes are working better than more traditional arrangements.

## The Challenge of Continuous Learning

Developing high-performance organizations requires changing our mental models of how organizations operate. Moving toward a continuous learning environment is a key challenge posed to high-performance organizations.

High-performance organizations embrace the concept of continuous learning. Continuous learning requires that organizations be open in their communications—sharing information and knowledge rather than protecting it. Continuous learning also means investing resources and time. If sustained, such an investment will reap great dividends.

Continuous learning begins with a clear vision shared among employees and a sense of where leverage can be exerted to change things for the better. Leadership does not simply sit at the peak of a tall command-and-control structure. Rather, leaders are in the business of helping their employees learn how to do things better. And leaders make certain that they are learning from employees at all times.

Rigid hierarchical organizations are usually the antithesis of continuous learning organizations. The process of work is fragmented, and few employees learn from each other. A command-and-control model derived from industrial processes and the military has been in place for many years.

A continuous learning process, however, can take hold in even the most structured organization where leadership is present. Because mental models and expectations are so crucial to the continuance of the old order, it is possible to change organizations by changing expectations of how things are supposed to work. This offers considerable hope for establishing high-performance organizations in government and clarifies the need to empower the people within an organization to change its operations.

Developing a shared vision and collaborative approaches between management and labor is even more important in the public sector, as we develop a deeper commitment to continuous learning. Unionization is more prevalent in the public sector than in the private sector. Although 12 percent of workers are unionized in the private sector, union membership reaches 40 percent of the public sector workforce. Because the unionized workforce represents such a large part of government, a working partnership between management and labor is essential from the start of any move toward high-performance organizations.

# WHAT IS REQUIRED TO BUILD A HIGH-PERFORMANCE ORGANIZATION?

If public sector organizations are interested in becoming high-performance workplaces, they will have to embrace and exert some fundamental tenets:

- Consistent, sustained leadership focused on high performance
- Willingness to develop performance measures
- Willingness to change whole organizations to provide higher quality and more appropriate services at equal or reduced costs
- Willingness to allocate resources to continuous learning

## Consistent and Sustained Leadership

Consistent, sustained leadership should focus on high performance. Indeed, a prerequisite for implementing a high-performance work organization is consistent and sustained leadership. Leadership involves several critical dimensions, including vision, commitment, inspiration, and the ability to facilitate change. Leaders must have a vision of the organization's future and communicate it effectively. They must be committed to making wholesale changes in the culture and processes of the organization and to sticking with those changes. And they must be able to inspire employees as well as the larger community to want to move toward being a high-performance organization.

With effective leadership, good ideas can penetrate established government processes and transform them. In a unionized workplace, having union leaders committed to the same goal adds immeasurably to the likelihood of success.

## Willingness to Develop Performance Measures

Incorporating performance measures into government operations will initially inspire some fear and resistance. Remember that performance measures are quantitative or qualitative tools for assessing whether policies or programs are contributing to the achievement of desirable outcomes or results. Leaders must be willing to work with stakeholders to establish baselines against which to measure progress and to set specific goals.

Without the ability to measure progress, high-performance workplace initiatives are like good intentions. They may feel better in the short run, but they will make little difference in the long term. Performance measurement systems are crucial to the ability of managers to remain accountable to elected leaders while decentralizing authority and responsibility and paring back inflexible command-and-control functions. (See Chapter Seven for a discussion of steps involved in creating performance measurement systems.)

## Willingness to Change Whole Organizations

Sometimes, whole organizations must change to provide higher quality and more appropriate services at equal or reduced costs. To reach high performance, all aspects of that organization eventually must be open to change. If a leader of an organization announces, for example, that several agencies or bureaus will adopt high-performance characteristics but does not agree to change the central management processes under which those agencies must operate, the experiment may never get off the ground.

Although change can be implemented incrementally, critical pieces of the change process must come together at the right time. Sequencing and coordination are critical. Take a state interagency team experimenting with self-organizing work teams. If the team requires computer networks to ease communications and performance measurement, the purchasing process must provide the computer networks in a timely manner. And training must be delivered in time to the work teams. Part of the process of change is to determine which of the incremental reforms are both necessary and sufficient to begin changing the entire system.

## Willingness to Allocate Resources to Continuous Learning

Many private companies recognize that continuous learning requires the allocation of substantial resources to education and training. Education and training are integrated into production processes. Government, however, too often views employee education and training as unnecessary or even as a luxury.

Increasingly, government managers are recognizing what union leaders have advocated for a long time—that education and training for front-line workers are necessities, not luxuries. This is particularly true if we are talking about changing the mental models from which we operate. Reorienting the way we think about our relationship to work, customers, and the external environment requires training and practice as much as changes in the way we perform work tasks.

When these attitudes are internalized by leaders and other stakeholders, the organization is well on its way to becoming a high-performance workplace. As this process proceeds, stakeholders will want to know how you are doing, what progress you are making, and whether you are being successful in your efforts of transformation.

## HOW DOES AN ORGANIZATION KNOW WHETHER IT IS BECOMING HIGH PERFORMING?

To create high-performance organizations, we need to determine how stakeholders would know when we are approaching that goal. In the private sector, it is relatively easy to determine whether an organization is performing well. Businesses have well-defined measures of performance. These include operating profit and return on investment as well as intermediate measures such as turnaround time, order response time, or inventory measures.

In government, a paucity of performance measures makes it difficult to determine whether an organization is performing. As a result, government leaders who want to improve performance need to develop four types of indicators. They must continue to monitor these indicators as the process of change toward high-performance organizations takes place. These include

- Better measures of performance
- Measures of improved performance
- Measures of internal organizational characteristics
- Measures of customer and stakeholder perceptions

High-performance organizations know how they are doing. They set quantifiable goals and measure their progress toward achieving them. By defining desirable outcomes and measuring whether conditions are getting better or worse, government employees can know how well they are performing. Are they are realizing the vision of the organization?

Government agencies are struggling to catch up to the private sector in its ability to measure performance. But some agencies are making great strides. Efforts to quantify results and develop meaningful performance measures are under way in state, local, and federal governments. Because of the lack of any track record in most government agencies in measuring outcomes, it will take time to develop effective measures.

## HOW LONG WILL IT TAKE?

Developing high-performance organizations takes sustained effort. The effort is likely to exceed the tenure of most elected officials. This implies that the change process itself must take on a life of its own. It must be pushed by incentives and other built-in motivators.

Instituting high-performance initiatives only to please the governor or mayor during the last year of their term probably will not have a lasting effect. If possible, those dedicated to creating high-performance organizations should do their best to institutionalize incentives and new processes that encourage and allow innovation to take place in the normal course of business.

At the same time, movement toward high performance can and should yield significant returns for elected officials in the short run. Progress must therefore be viewed in both the short and longer term. Be on the lookout for low-hanging fruit that can yield important progress in the short term. Celebrate your victories, and be sure to spread the word to stakeholders.

For example, many pockets of innovation can be created to introduce the concepts of high-performance workplaces into the larger organization. These can be quite visible and can have significant public appeal. The application of these concepts can stimulate and enhance their attractiveness to other parts of the larger organization and can, in this way, spread and build on success. Elected leaders can call attention to the need for change, put in place a change process, and realize some short-term benefits. In the longer term, the entire organization must be involved in the process and committed to its principles if the organization is to be truly high performing. The role of management and employees becomes one of institutionalizing high-performance characteristics over the longer term.

In the words of one public policy advocate, the long-term role is often dark and lonely work. It is by no means automatic and inevitable. It is fraught with setbacks, shifts in support, and opportunities to get wildly off track. To help guide you along this difficult road, the next chapters outline steps that you will need to go through. And we offer a range of tools and tips to aid you on your way.

The elements of a strategic planning and change process are divided into four main components. These include

- Chapter Four: Preparing the Way for Change
- Chapter Five: Crafting Your Vision, Mission, and Values
- Chapter Six: Conducting Useful Organizational Assessments
- Chapter Seven: Designing a Results-Driven Plan for Change

# CHAPTER THREE

# Mastering the Politics of Change

C hanging any organization, public or private, requires attention to the organizational politics of change. In the public sector, the politics of change is often more complex than in the business world. Authority to make decisions is shared under our traditional system of checks and balances. Major changes necessitate securing approval of at least the executive and legislative branches and sometimes defending them before courts of law and the court of public opinion.

The scope of decision-making authority, for civil servants and elected and appointed leadership alike, is circumscribed by law, regulation, and administrative procedure. Requirements for public notice and participation are specified. Achieving change means altering the status quo. To secure it, change agents must plan ahead.

In many cases, such as changing budget processes or personnel rules, you must be able to orchestrate sustained cooperation across offices within your organization and with other agencies who exercise administrative and oversight responsibilities.

Champions of change must also master the nuances of the larger world of politics and the politics of their own organizations. In this section, we explore a series of considerations related to both internal and external politics. We begin by proposing some rules of the road you can use to guide your way through the political maze.

## SUMMARY OF RULES OF THE ROAD

Based on experience in government, we offer eight rules of the road for taking politics into consideration in the process of change.

1. Nearly every move you make will be interpreted by someone as having a political motivation.
2. In fact, if your goal is to improve government, your actions will have political implications.
3. People within your organization are wary of change.
4. Changing the rules requires that you do not go back to the bad old days.
5. Change within your organization will be watched carefully by interest groups, both inside and outside your organization.
6. Leadership in the public sector is perishable.
7. Opportunities to make significant change are greatly influenced by political, policy, and other cycles.
8. Above all else, political leaders hate surprises.

## THE RULES IN DETAIL

Each effort to reach for high performance must find its own path through political roadblocks. The rules, however, can serve as a general map to help steer you around major hazards.

1. *Nearly every move you make will be interpreted by someone as having a political motivation.* Every important move, indeed, does have political implications. All governmental organizations got the way they are because of decisions by political leaders and their close subordinates. Public organizations develop a political history that is known to some but not to all.

Seasoned practitioners know that in government you should never assume that the status quo is an accident. Things are the way they are because somebody at sometime wanted them that way. In the public sector, you act at some peril if you do not first understand why the status quo developed and who wanted it that way.

Procurement by state agencies in Maryland, for example, is governed by fairly onerous requirements. It frequently takes six months or more to issue a contract or to purchase materials, even when the expenditures are relatively small. Few businesses could thrive under such restrictions. And for Maryland agencies, these limits sometimes hinder high performance. But they are not an accident.

The stringency of the process was a response to a series of high-profile scandals in the state. Over the years, the media chronicled cases of payoffs to government officials and the abuse of power in state contracting or procurement. Limitations on discretion, the further dilution of authority for procurement, and disclosure requirements were the intended result.

Our democratic system demands that politicians be responsive to public demands. Public agencies and the people who manage them must respond to changes in public priorities and to the politicians who face them most directly. If you want to streamline middle management, there will certainly be a legislator, legislative staff member, or some interest group who will be most interested in what you intend to do and how you plan to do it. Even a decision to survey public attitudes or customer satisfaction may be viewed by someone as your way of gaining politically useful information at the taxpayer's expense.

You need a clear-eyed understanding of the political impact your intended changes may have. How will they be viewed by elected and other officials who must provide license or approval? Engage them early and often so that they have the clearest possible understanding of what you intend to do. Outline how you hope to do it. If you cannot arrange an interview with them directly, approach others who work closely with them. The special assistant, public information officer, lobbyist, or even a seasoned reporter on your state capitol or city hall beat can be a valuable source of insight. Bounce your strategies off them and welcome constructive criticism.

To begin, you need to recognize that politicians and top-level appointees adopt limited agendas. They have set priorities to focus their efforts. Fit your plan into their priorities, and you are well along the way to winning their attention. And getting their attention is the first step toward earning their support.

2. *In fact, if your goal is to improve government, your actions will have political implications.* Nearly all your actions aimed at achieving

high performance will be interpreted politically. But do not be frozen into inaction by that prospect. There may well be "good" politics to support changes you want. Governors, council members, and political appointees across the country have embraced the goals of government reinvention. Candidates and incumbents tout plans for making the public sector more productive, efficient, and in touch with its customers. Even those who strongly believe the world needs less government can see the value of making your organization more efficient and effective.

Whether you are a front-line employee who believes in change, an agency director, or a budget analyst, remember that one important currency in politics is to make the person you are working for look good. Power and prestige are affected by positive public recognition for a job well done. Before you make changes in your organization, you must consider how they will be perceived by other political actors.

If you are in the executive branch, do not forget the legislators. Reach out to the press and public. Outreach to the full range of players in the public arena is an opportunity to get your message defined clearly and effectively. Communications and outreach are as professionalized and specialized as are the jobs of a legal counsel or an auditor. You have to invest in it and use it at the right time. Far too often, agency staff enlist the support of public information specialists as a final step in launching change. Or they are called upon only in response to a crisis. Bring them in from the start, and you will strengthen your team's ability to get the job done right.

3. *People within your organization are wary of change.* Political leaders are firmly on the bandwagon for many organizational change strategies. Many have moved political mountains to create more effective, responsive, and efficient agencies. However, there are too many cases in which organizational and systemic change were used symbolically. Some leaders may want to signal to the legislature, the press, powerful stakeholders, or directly to the voters that they have a new way of thinking about the process of governance. Or they may simply seek a push in the polls that attacks on inefficiency or waste often yield.

Sometimes, resistance to change from staff is the result of a history of waves of changes that may have been more cosmetic than real. Past "reorganizations" that were nine parts appearance to one part performance have buffeted many agencies. Overcoming deep skepticism will be part of the price of producing the change you desire.

Support for your new ideas is likely to be shallow indeed unless you can overcome it.

People at all levels of an organization can be unsettled by change. Their concerns—even their misperceptions—are legitimate. Build in as many opportunities as possible to communicate with them. Talk with them, not to them. Be clear about why you seek change. Describe how you plan to bring it about. Discuss openly how change may affect them, and enlist their energy and ideas to support the cause.

4. *Changing the rules requires that you do not go back to the bad old days.* Many barriers to change started out as reasonable protections against whimsical or malicious political change. Going back to the bad old days is not an option. Civil service, purchasing regulations, even rules for filling out employee time sheets can impede performance in the public sector.

But many of these barriers were, in fact, reforms when they were first adopted. People wanted protection from nepotism, racial discrimination, or political corruption. It may be hard to dismiss an incompetent teacher today precisely because it was too easy to drop a good teacher to favor a political hack.

When you plan to change the operating procedures or rules of your organization or when you appeal to a central management agency for greater flexibility, remember the legitimate reasons for those rules. They may now be obsolete, or you may have a better procedure for protecting against abuse while striving for performance. But you will have to prove to many others, such as colleagues, employees, interest groups, and politicians, that your reforms are not simply an invitation to return to the bad old days.

For example, Oregon recently petitioned the U.S. Department of Labor to substitute state procurement processes for the federal requirements under the Job Training Partnership Act (JTPA). Generally, the protections and procedures are comparable. And Oregon has a well-earned reputation as a good-government, clean-politics state. But there were objections to the state's request. State procedures were in many ways more than adequate. Discussions among state and federal officials, however, surfaced differences between the two sets of rules that had important policy implications. Oregon's procurement system permits sole-source contracting with local governments. Federal officials were concerned that this provision might limit the ability of community-based organizations to compete for contracts. Would there be a level playing field in JTPA contracting?

Oregon simply wanted to streamline procurement. But to do so, they had to convince federal officials that they would not put non-profit agencies at a disadvantage. The Department of Labor had to be satisfied that the federal goal of engaging a wider array of organizations in providing services would be met under state procedures.

5. *Change within your organization will be watched carefully by interest groups, both inside and outside your organization.* Government agencies operate under a microscope. People in and outside government will watch closely as your operations change. They will be looking for both good and bad news.

Unions, for example, will watch exceedingly closely to make sure that employees are not mistreated. They are vigilant to ensure that contracts are not violated during change. Legislators and their staff will monitor your changes to make sure that their districts or important interest groups are not adversely affected.

Many people and organizations will be tireless in watching out for their interests any time a public organization decides to change something. If your changes are serious or wide ranging, those people and organizations will react strongly. When this happens, you and your political leaders will begin to receive feedback signals.

Make sure you have the capacity and sensitivity to pick up these signals. Listen carefully to them all, even though you need not take them all seriously. You may not change your plans as a result. But it will help to keep your head up and ears open. An ostrich may feel safe with its head in the sand, but taking that position opens the poor bird to unanticipated attacks.

Doug Ross was a successful innovator as the head of Michigan's Department of Commerce and the U.S. Employment and Training Administration. He offers an important insight. Leaders, in his view, are distinguished by their ability to craft an effective demand for change. Your vantage point may be from the top of an agency or from middle management; in either case, there is a constant need to create solutions to pressing problems of the day. Rarely, however, is sufficient attention paid to finding and using the levers that can help create a demand for change by the public or elected leaders. You may never become a spin-master, a public relations expert, or a media darling, but you can build your capacity to get your message across to both internal and external audiences.

6. *Leadership in the public sector is perishable.* Turnover of leaders is not unique to the government, but we may have perfected it as an

art form. The rapid pace of leadership changes is a fact of life for most public organizations. Building a career often means moving up or out. Reductions in force and early retirement packages thin the leadership corps, usually when the challenges of leadership are greatest. Appointees slip from the public spotlight back into careers in the private sector. Elections are won and lost.

Even when leadership is not durable, change still can flourish. Maintaining support for change requires constant vigilance—and a strategic view. You may be in the trenches for the duration or an appointee with a hitch that may last only twenty-four months. In any case, you can take steps to build durability into the change process.

Oregon can boast startling success in sustaining a far-reaching change process (Macy, 1997). The effort began in 1988 and 1989 as the state pioneered a strategic planning process with a strong emphasis on results. Thousands of citizens helped set goals; some 270 benchmarks were devised to regularly measure progress toward those goals. Governor Kitzhaber is the third chief executive to embrace the benchmarking process. Nine years after the initial steps in developing the benchmarks, he has overseen a thorough assessment and update of the strategic plan and benchmarks (Oregon Progress Board, 1997).

Few states are willing to develop a comprehensive vision of their future. Fewer still build a process that endures more than a few years. Some keys to building staying power into the change process in Oregon include

> *Commitment of top leadership.* From its inception, top-level leaders from the state and local governments, private sector, community groups, and academia shepherded the development of Oregon's strategic plan. It is a reinforcing cycle. Because top officials led the process, it had credibility from the start.
>
> *Public engagement.* Public participation builds broad public ownership. Public review and comment were integral to every step on the way to developing the benchmarks (Oregon Progress Board, 1993). To complete the third biennial benchmark report in 1995, for example, Oregon conducted polling of public values and priorities. Over two thousand people participated in twenty-nine town hall meetings. Direct mail to twelve thousand people solicited their comments. And some fifty thousand copies of earlier benchmark reports were disseminated (Macy, 1997; Popovich, 1996).
>
> *Creating a caretaker.* The Oregon Progress Board was created by statute in 1989 to serve as the long-term caretaker of the strategic vision.

A process launched by the executive was formally recognized by the legislature. Staff and budget were allocated, and the board's roles were codified. The governors, who chair the board, have been active participants.

*Regular updating and reporting.* State law also mandated reports to the legislature every two years to update the plan. The updates not only refresh the plan, they also present regular opportunities to renew the commitment to its principles.

*Practice, practice, practice.* Without constant practice, a musician's skills quickly atrophy. Unless a change process is converted into practical action, it is of little value. In 1992, Governor Barbara Roberts used the benchmarks to guide the state's response to a serious and growing fiscal challenge (Popovich, 1996). Governor Roberts directed all state agencies to give priority to critical near-term benchmarks in developing their budget proposals. And the benchmarks were directly tied to a series of budget initiatives such as strengthening job-related education, improving stream flows and water quality, and limiting urban congestion (Oregon Progress Board, 1993).

*Shaping organizational cultures.* Because they are useful, the benchmarks are used. The level of knowledge of and commitment to the benchmarks in Oregon is impressive. In many agencies, commitment has spread beyond policymakers to career managers and many frontline employees. And advocates champion benchmarks in their areas of interest.

7. *Opportunities to make significant change are influenced by political, policy, and election cycles.* To paraphrase legendary football coach Vince Lombardi, timing isn't everything; it's the only thing. Although that is not always true, getting the timing right is important enough to think of it that way.

Building a change effort is a bit like playing in a very large jazz ensemble. You start with a tempo in mind. The players begin to lay down some melody based on it. But you must listen closely. As soloists let loose or the rhythm section hits a groove, there will be changes. You have the dual responsibility of keeping the beat moving forward while responding to the tempo changes.

Some rules of timing should be obvious. For example, an agency head will face greater resistance if they start reinventing their agency in their final year in office. Line managers seldom can get attention for their detailed reform plans from politicians in election season. Nor are you likely to win approval for streamlining onerous procurement procedures if the central office is struggling with a barrage of contracting abuse stories. But even in these cases, the rules are not immutable. That is why getting the timing right is tricky.

We do not suggest that you do nothing if you think key cycles do not seem to align perfectly. At every point in the political process, for example, there is an opportunity to move forward in some way.

8. *Above all else, political leaders hate surprises.* They may abhor losing a legislative battle or an election more. But to politicians, surprise is too often a step on the road to some defeat or loss.

If you make changes they do not know about, and if any of these backfire, they may well be called on to make a painful decision. They will face deciding whether to defend or halt your efforts, to discipline you, or maybe even to fire you. It is better to keep them informed all along the way of any plans you have for change. Detail your rationales. And describe how they fit into political, legislative, and budget cycles. Then if anything does go wrong, at least they will know what is going on.

Ensuring that elected or other leaders are not blindsided is a major challenge. But it is an absolute requirement for the kind of changes you will be contemplating. Make sure that you have good communications links with leaders whose support you will need. A well-informed leader is far less likely to make an ill-conceived decision. They become more confident supporters. And they can help right you if you hit turbulence along the path to change.

## KEEPING THE POLITICAL FAITH

Regardless of their ideological leanings, most leaders in politically sensitive jobs want to see government work better. They are aware of productivity and service quality gains in other agencies and the private sector. They would like to emulate or exceed them. As a result, they are very likely to support reasonable plans for change.

Adhere to the rules of the road just discussed, and you will smooth the way toward becoming a high-performance organization. If you demonstrate real achievement, make sure that credit for victories is widely shared. Political leaders can be your closest allies. Many are willing to take real risks and to devote their energies and resources to achieve better performance. Demonstrating that you are sensitive to their needs simply builds their inclination and their capacity to support your changes.

# PART TWO

# Key Steps in Planning for High Performance

# CHAPTER FOUR

# Preparing the Way for Change

How and where do you start? As a manager, you are responsible for overseeing programs and services, and you have some latitude in the way you operate them. As an employee, you have ideas on how you and your colleagues can work smarter, be more responsive, and do a better job of linking your operations to the organization's overall goals. As an elected official, you may feel the need to reorient major functions of government.

This chapter discusses a variety of approaches and steps you can take to tackle one of your greatest challenges—getting started. In any change process, this can be one of the most difficult aspects. How do we know where to begin? What exactly do we want to accomplish? Whom can we look to for support? What opportunities exist to build upon? What obstacles are we likely to encounter?

Implementing changes to build high performance into your organization seems like a daunting challenge. To make the change process manageable, you will need to do some strategic thinking. A strategic plan cannot guide your every move, but it will help set the parameters of the changes you will seek. And by taking some time to think it through first, you can better anticipate both barriers to and opportunities for meeting your goals.

Organizations can change without a plan. Most organisms in the natural world do exactly that. Some management gurus advocate changing organizations without strategic plans. They focus on building the ability to change into the organization itself and allowing it to respond to its environment. When we consider planless change, however, you should recognize the risks. Scientists estimate that 99 percent of all species that developed through evolution have become extinct.

In the public sector at least, our chances for enduring change appear to be improved if we clarify our purpose and develop strategies for achieving it. This does not mean that we need to invest enormous amounts of time and resources into a complex, long-winded strategic planning document. That might provide an easy excuse to do nothing or to leave the problem to the agency's planners.

## GETTING STRATEGIC

There is value, however, in taking some time to get strategic. You need to anticipate the issues and problems that you will face, consider options for addressing them, select strategies, and continually reevaluate and improve your efforts.

The strategic change process is not necessarily linear, and it is likely to be iterative. To start, you will probably take the first steps on your own or with a small number of people. You may well find that you need to focus on two or more steps simultaneously. And sooner or later, you will need to broaden the partners in your change process to include more stakeholders. As the circle widens, including new participants will require repeating some steps.

Your change process will be unique. If it is to work, it cannot be drawn in its entirety from any other government's effort. But you have much experience to draw from. Remember, however, that you will need to take care to customize the steps in the process to your unique needs along the way.

Experience in the private sector and among other government organizations indicates that the process of change must be continuous. You might think of it as a work in progress, like a spiral, cycling toward continuous improvement.

Taking a strategic view need not involve an elaborate or formal planning process. Much depends on whether the organization already has some elements in place. If you already have a well-developed mission statement or the agency has proposed measurable goals, you can build on that base.

Formal declarations that change is coming are sometimes not necessary. They may create more angst and resistance than necessary. Some of the successful innovations in government have sprung from instilling elements of high-performance organizations into the day-to-day life and culture of the organization—piece by piece and without fanfare but with the benefit of strategic thinking and planning.

Regardless of your approach, creating high-performance organizations is hard work and it takes time. Change can happen at many different levels of the organization at once. It can happen at a strategic and policy level when funds are assigned. And it can happen at an operational level when individual work is redesigned or decision-making authority is reassigned. It can begin with you, regardless of where you are in the organization.

## FOUR FIRST STEPS

No matter where you begin, it will be helpful to familiarize yourself with the four different types of activities that will help you get started: (1) clarifying your purpose, (2) understanding the environment, (3) engaging stakeholders, and (4) building commitment to change.

Your first steps are aimed at helping you establish the need for change, understand the parameters within which you must work, identify all those who will be important to the change process, and get enough of the right people on board so that you can go to the next step.

### Clarifying Your Purpose

Whether they excitedly embrace or merely tolerate changes, people in your organization and those who monitor it want to know that the organization is changing and where it is going.

At this step, you need to clarify ideas about the type of high-performance organization you want to create and why you want to create it. It involves establishing the need for change in your own mind and in the mind of others who share the vision of a high-performance organization.

Clarity of purpose may well be the one constant across all high-performance organizations. Everyone in the organization, from leaders to front-line workers, understands what the organization exists to accomplish. Similarly, the change process must have a clear purpose—one related to the mission of the organization as a whole. Those who have made the transition to high-performance organizations underscore the need to be clear about where the organization is going and why.

Clarifying the purpose of the change process will involve some work. The city manager's office in Hampton, Virginia, offers a good example of one approach to clarifying an organization's purpose. Ten years ago that office received a clear challenge from the city council to dramatically improve performance. A new city manager was hired to do new things quickly and to do them well. To figure out what they would do and how they would go about it, the manager and three assistants spent a week away from the office thinking about and discussing their options. They discussed the elements of the high-performance organization they wanted to create. They asked themselves: Did they have the right people and the right structure? They felt that they had the right people, but they were not so sure they had the right structure. They had a standard government hierarchy, with department heads reporting to three assistant city managers who ran the day-to-day operations. Because the assistants were very individualistic and competent, they ran three essentially separate operations. One assistant city manager kept a log for a month and found that 75 percent of his time was spent dealing with department-specific issues. He did not think this was the value he should be adding to the organization. He wanted to step back, create a vision, and think about how to get there. He wanted to be more strategic. This process helped Hampton focus on where they wanted to go, what the strengths and weaknesses of their current operation were, and what they needed to change. The retreat led to some advances. They helped develop a clear mission statement. Operations were restructured to enable them to accomplish this mission. And they built employee involvement into the entire process. It began with developing a clearer vision of what they wanted and how they would proceed.

Richmond, Virginia, is only about a sixty-minute drive from Hampton. But their latest round of change started from a very different point. Through the efforts of Robert Bobb, the city manager, and the city council members, Richmond already had a strategic plan complete with specific goals. Over the last year, however, city leaders re-doubled their attention to improving public safety. Bobb also used a retreat to focus Richmond's efforts to tackle these challenges. Both the city manager and the chief of police had already concluded that it would take more than just the police to achieve their public safety goals. It would take the cooperative efforts of all agencies. There could not be a single solution or step adequate to solve the problem. There could be—in fact there must be—dozens of steps. To develop them, sixty-five of the top managers from city agencies participated in a two-day, off-site session focused exclusively on this issue. And rather than starting with an abstract discussion, they used a story to concentrate the group on real problems and to develop solutions that would really work. The story, a real-world incident response report, detailed the series of problems encountered by front-line officers in responding to a recent call.

On September [X], 1996, officers were dispatched to [specific address], a small apartment 200 feet to the rear of this address. This address is an abandoned, boarded-up, "salt box" house known in the neighborhood as a local crack house. The house has been boarded and reboarded several times, but it continues to be used for illegal purposes. Response was delayed in part because there was no address indicated on the house, and overgrown trees along the street were obstructing views of any activity going on at the house.

Upon arrival, the officers found a 20 month old infant female in complete code [unconscious and not breathing]. They were met at the door by an obviously pregnant female of about 25 years of age who reeked of alcohol and appeared to be intoxicated. Officers performed mouth-to-mouth and chest compressions in an effort to revive the baby. Neither officer used protective devices as required by policy, having left their kits in their vehicles. The baby was later transported to hospital and was pronounced dead. The cause of death is unknown at this time. Three other children of school age were also found in the apartment. They were later fostered through Child Protective Services by follow-up detectives due to abhorrent living conditions and their neglected hygiene.

Records indicate that the officers have responded to violent incidents at this location over the past two weeks. Additionally, two drug related homicides have been attributed to the street in front of this location over the past couple of years. Responding officers were not aware of these previous incidents at the time of their response.

## Examples of Richmond's Public Safety Strategy Implementation Steps

Through their discussion at the retreat and follow-on efforts, city leaders developed a strategy for responding to these challenges. Their proposals:

- Support officers in high-crime areas with proactive advance teams.
- Develop a second-responder team—a twenty-four-hour, on-call human services team.
- Develop a crisis coordination team to provide comprehensive service response. Focus on multiple-response addresses.
- Target enforcement on drug offenses, weapons violations, and vice offenses.
- Reallocate resources in agencies to prioritize police-initiated requests.
- Prioritize demolition in high-crime areas.
- Prioritize hot spots and complete an assessment of needs for changing the physical environment in high-crime areas.
- Correct environmental conditions in fifteen hot spots.
- Enforce the posted address law.

Richmond and Hampton started at different points. They used different techniques. But, in the end, they tackled many similar steps in taking a strategic view of their change processes.

We suggest that you begin your efforts by thinking through two important steps first:

1. Review the characteristics of high-performance organizations.
2. Assess the strengths and weaknesses of your current organization.

*Review the characteristics of high-performance organizations.* A discussion of the characteristics of high-performance organizations and some of the reasons that momentum is building in the public sector for this transition is included in Chapter One. In Chapter Two, you will find a discussion of the challenges public sector agencies face in moving toward high performance. A review of these materials by you and others interested in embarking on this process will be helpful in setting the stage for change. The sample questionnaire can be used either as a checklist or a survey to assess your current organization (see Exhibits 4.1 and 4.2).

*Assess the strengths and weaknesses of your current organization.* Based on your new knowledge about high-performance organizations, we suggest that you review your own organization. This will help you identify where your organization has some elements to build on, as well as clear weaknesses to address. You can do this by comparing how your organization works with the characteristics of high-performance organizations found in Chapter One.

Your goal is to get an overview of where your organization now stands. Later, you will want to complete a full-scale assessment (see Chapter Six). The initial assessment will yield a snapshot or working profile you can use as a starting point.

If your organization has no way of measuring results, for example, you will need to work on a results orientation. If your headquarters staff is not in tune with the needs of the agency's customers, this will be an area where the change process must focus. You will know whether or not your organization has a clear view of its purpose. And you will have an understanding of its flexibility and ability to adjust to change and how competitive it is in terms of its performance.

After you have taken a look at how your organization stacks up with high-performing ones, you can make your first decisions about the areas on which to focus. You should consider making a simple list of the characteristics of high-performing organizations in which there are opportunities for improvement. Then, build your planning and change process around that list.

## UNDERSTANDING THE ENVIRONMENT

The next step in this planning process is to understand the political, economic, and cultural environment in which your organization operates. This will help you understand some of the factors that will constrain or enable your organization to move toward high performance. This step is often referred to as an *environmental scan.*

An environmental scan is an assessment of key elements of the environment in which your organization operates that currently influence the way your organization works. These include elements that

*Introduction:* Earlier today we reviewed characteristics common to high-performance organizations. This survey asks you and your colleagues to assess where our organization currently stands on this scale. It is also an early opportunity to share some of your ideas about where and how we can change to better meet our mission and reach our full high-performance potential. The survey will take only about 10–15 minutes to complete, but your ideas will be important to how we work together to improve performance.

1. First, we would like some information about you and your job. Please check all the categories below that apply to you.

   Job-Related Activities:

   __ Fiscal/Budget __ Policy __ Administration __ Support

   __ Program Management __ Evaluation/Auditing __ Personnel

   __ Service Delivery __ Public Outreach __ Information Tech

   __ Procurement __ Building Services

   Other: _____

2. How well do you think our agency is doing right now on these characteristics? We ...

|  | Poor |  | Average |  | Good |
|---|---|---|---|---|---|
| a. Are clear on our mission | 1 | 2 | 3 | 4 | 5 |
| b. Define outcomes | 1 | 2 | 3 | 4 | 5 |
| c. Focus on results that matter | 1 | 2 | 3 | 4 | 5 |
| d. Empower employees | 1 | 2 | 3 | 4 | 5 |
| e. Motivate and inspire employees to succeed | 1 | 2 | 3 | 4 | 5 |
| f. Are flexible and adjust to changing conditions | 1 | 2 | 3 | 4 | 5 |
| g. Are competitive in terms of performance | 1 | 2 | 3 | 4 | 5 |
| h. Restructure work processes to meet customer needs | 1 | 2 | 3 | 4 | 5 |
| i. Maintain communications with stakeholders | 1 | 2 | 3 | 4 | 5 |

3. What ideas do you have for making changes that could help improve your effectiveness and the performance of our agency?

4. What next steps do you think you can help us take to achieve those goals? What role would you be willing to play?

**Exhibit 4.1.    High-Performance Characteristics: A Sample Survey.**

---

*Build a Base of Understanding:* Take time to review the characteristics of high-performance organizations thoroughly before using the survey. Schedule plenty of time for discussion.

*Make It Real:* Use examples to illustrate each of the characteristics. You can draw on the cases in Chapter One. Or, better still, you can use examples from your agency or others like it. We have found that examples from the same level of government and comparable agencies have the most impact.

*Create an Environment for Honest Assessment:* Be clear about why you are asking for the information and how you plan to use it. The survey can be anonymous, or you could ask people to give their name and affiliation.

*Disaggregate the Results:* Break out results and look at the range of ratings. Average scores on Question 2 can tell you a lot. But looking at the frequency of each rating (1, 2, 3, 4, and 5) can tell you even more.

*Share the Results:* Complete the analysis of the survey, summarize the findings, and report back promptly to the participants.

*Identify Next Steps:* If at all possible, clarify next steps, a time line, and assignments when you report the survey results. This can help maintain momentum and take advantage of volunteers who identify themselves early in the process.

*Clarify Desired Qualities:* After a first-cut comparison of your organization to those that are high performing, a number of areas of concentration in your own organization should become obvious.

---

**Exhibit 4.2.    Some Tips for Using the Sample Survey.**


are *economic and demographic, social, political, cultural, historical,* or *technological.*

An environmental scan is also an assessment of how these factors differ by geographical area. For example, it may be important for you to understand cultural or political differences among households and neighborhoods if your organization exists at the local government level. If you work at the state level, you will want to look at the city and county levels. You should also consider national and international factors that may influence your environment.

John Mercer, the former mayor of Sunnyvale, California, found that understanding differences in culture in the public sector was an important step in his efforts to transform his city. He reflects that the structure, traditions, and expectations of government differ by region. Eastern cities are more likely to have partisan elections, and politics plays a larger role in decision making. In the West, government is more often viewed as responsible for providing high-quality services as proficiently as possible. In the Southwest and the West, the council manager form of government predominates on the local level. There are often no local partisan elections, and nonpartisan governmental structures more often emphasize professionalism. District elections have a real impact on the way city governments perform. When politics intervenes—wards, partisan alliances, and patronage—government's focus on performance by professional standards may be lessened. Mercer maintains that the fundamental structure of government is at issue here. The structure itself sends a message of what government is about and what it wants. Culture, expectations, and decision-making styles affect structure. And they should be taken into account in understanding the environment for change.

A thorough understanding of all these factors impinging on your organization would take many weeks or months to acquire. For the purposes of planning for change, however, a scan of these factors can be accomplished quickly. Where data exist, examine how they have changed over time and any projections you might have for the future. When no data are readily available, use the opinions of valued members of your organization and focus groups of outsiders (see Exhibits 4.3 and 4.4).

Use the environmental scanning process to educate members of your own organization about the underlying premises with which you work. If your mission is to find jobs for the unemployed, for example, how can you cope with changing economic, social, and demographic conditions? Are the political constraints placed on your organization such that it cannot possibly succeed? However, what social and economic conditions can be leveraged to help you accomplish your mission?

Part of an environmental scan is to examine the external and internal forces that can help your organization change. To make this part of the assessment, questions that should be answered include the following:

> Who is likely to support—politically, financially, or otherwise—your effort?
>
> Who is likely to resist? Why?
>
> Are other organizations in the midst of similar change processes? If so, how did they get started? What is working well and what is not?
>
> Is there adequate support available, such as funding, staffing, and the attention of top leaders for developing and implementing a change process?
>
> Does the system allow reassignment of people to work on an effort such as this? Will the current personnel policies allow you to change the responsibilities of some jobs?

- What factors, trends, and conditions are likely to have the greatest impact on your organization and its ability to carry out its mission?
- What are the implications of these trends, both positive and negative, for your organization?
- Who are the customers of your organization?
- How has the customers' environment been changing?
- How effective has your organization been in achieving desired results for these customers?
- What forces are influencing the ability of your organization to serve your customers?

**Exhibit 4.3.   The Environmental Scan: Guiding Questions.**

*Focus Your Time Horizon:* How far back or forward do you want to look? A year or two is likely to be too short to reveal enduring trends. At the same time, five-to-ten-year spans tend to conceal more than they reveal.

*Explore Feedback Loops:* Your organization is greatly influenced by its environment. But your organization also affects its environment. You may find some surprising strengths and weaknesses by taking this tack.

*Concentrate on Results:* You may want to look at how inputs such as budget and staffing have changed. But you should pay equal or greater attention to end results. A public works department may track the number of lane miles that meet or fall below engineering standards. But if the ultimate goal is highway safety or moving people efficiently, accident rates or levels of congestion on key highways may be better indicators.

*Go Beyond Averages:* Lake Wobegon's children, Garrison Keillor reports, are all above average. That is a justifiable point of pride for his mythical Minnesota village. But it is not a useful statistic if your job is to detail the children's changing needs for instruction and training. In some cases, attempting to understand how conditions are everywhere does not tell much about how they are anywhere. If your agency is charged with implementing welfare reform across the state, for example, you may concentrate on developing a detailed environmental scan on a handful of specific places. You may learn much more by understanding well the similarities and differences between a depressed inner-city neighborhood, a growing suburb, and a rural enclave battered by the departure of a major employer.

*Value Input from the Front Lines:* Statistics are essential to documenting current conditions and putting trends into scale. But do not let numbers numb your process. Some of the most important insights will come from interviewing your agency's front-line workers. They will often perceive new trends before they become statistically significant.

*Probe for Causes:* Begin to pull together and test ideas about why trends are shifting. Is a shift in conditions, for example, an aberration or a harbinger of greater changes ahead? This is when input from front-line staff will be particularly important in interpreting the information you have developed.

**Exhibit 4.4.   Some Tips for Environmental Scanning.**

Understanding the environment wherein you will plan and execute a process of change is an essential prerequisite to moving forward. Although you should be thorough, you can begin to move forward on other steps in the process even before you are satisfied that every possible element of the environment has been fully considered and documented. Before moving forward, however, you should have developed a clear view of most of the constraints and opportunities. That will keep you from being blindsided about issues or problems you will inevitably face in making the shift to high performance.

## IDENTIFYING STAKEHOLDERS

Changes in your organization affect your clients—those who depend on its services. Changes will affect every employee. But the effects, particularly in public agencies, extend far beyond those two groups. There are others inside government, both within and beyond the executive branch, whose support you will need to authorize and fund the changes.

Developing a stakeholder analysis requires your effort to identify all those persons and organizations who have a stake in any changes made in your organization. The stakeholder analysis reminds us of who cares about how our organization works. Key legislators, political executives and their staffs, unions, special interest groups, nonprofit service providers, contractors, and many others can be stakeholders in the performance of a government organization.

Some stakeholders will be receptive to change. Others will have powerful motives to resist change. All are more likely to become barriers to change if they are left out of the change process.

Your task will be to make a list of everyone who is affected by your organization or who has an interest in its success. By systematically identifying all those with a stake in either making change in the organization or keeping it the way it is, you will have a better idea of who to involve at the early stage of your process.

Deciding who to involve, how to involve them, and when to do it is a difficult call, however. You must be able to make some assessment of which stakeholders are likely to support the move and which may try to kill it. Then you will have to decide which stakeholders can help you build a critical mass of support, which can sustain action even in the face of opposition.

In Ohio's state government, a small group of people interested in improving services to families and children managed to garner some federal and foundation funds for this purpose through the Council of Governors' Policy Advisors (Chynoweth and Dyer, 1991). The working group met and made a first-cut listing of the stakeholders who should be involved in the process. They assembled the team and took them to a three-day working session out of the state. At the end of that session, the group decided that it needed to expand the list of state representatives involved in the process and extend involvement to local providers and the private sector. They also decided it was time to engage the governor in their efforts. His support became critical when an interest group mounted a statewide effort to derail the project. By pulling the governor and a larger group into the change process early and often, they had a reservoir of support to keep the effort moving forward.

By using the stakeholder analysis process as an iterative one, you can build commitment while you are bringing into the process the individuals and organizations necessary for change to occur. You could begin with a small, core group to meet and help define the initial parameters of the plan. This group may lead to a broader steering group responsible for guiding the effort. By systematically expanding your base of support, you can weather the storms that will undoubtedly form.

## BUILDING COMMITMENT TO CHANGE

You should use the strategic planning process itself to build a commitment for change. This implies that the process must be broadly conceived, taking advantage of every opportunity to involve stakeholders as the plans for change are developed.

Whether you are an appointed or elected leader of an organization or one of the workers, allies will be necessary even to begin the process of changing toward a high-performance organization. Getting started requires that these allies be recruited and that their opinions, concerns, and observations be considered carefully.

Some of these allies will be identified through the stakeholder analysis. Others will have to be sought out through other processes. Virtually all those in government who have worked on improving their organizations based on high-performance principles stress that a general commitment to change must be built as the process proceeds.

One person acting alone, even a charismatic leader, will not change a government organization. But one person can begin a process that can have profound effects on an organization.

In developing a commitment to change, you should consider the following three steps. They may seem obvious and somewhat pedestrian, but experience shows that skipping over these tasks can doom your aspirations for effective change:

1. Develop a core group of supporters.

2. Spread the word.

3. Let the key players know you value their advice.

1. *Develop a core group of supporters.* You will need to develop a group of people who can help you with your effort. You may do this informally through a group of interested associates, or you may choose a more formal steering group. It is likely that you will move from one strategy to the next as the process evolves.

One state university teacher became interested in the process of reinvention. He began by reading the literature and going to seminars on the subject. Over time, he recruited one of his peers to the effort. Together, they persuaded their boss and other colleagues to form a steering group. And they began an educational process on high performance for a wider circle of colleagues. They shared written material, brought in speakers, and interviewed consultants until they had built up enough commitment to move forward.

This university example illustrates how a core group of supporters can be formed by one employee, even one without management responsibilities. In the Hampton case, the city manager created his own core group of supporters by involving his three deputies in helping to clarify their purpose, understand their environment, and decide how to proceed. In both examples, an informal process led to a more formalized and broader-based effort to institute change.

2. *Spread the word.* Once you have established a group to support the change effort, you should begin the educational process in earnest. Expand your network and build a larger group to support change.

Ideally, as you build this larger group, you should bring in people in positions of authority to effect change. If you are a manager, you should bring in workers and persons with varying interests, thereby expanding involvement to include more and more stakeholders.

With this larger group, you should revisit the work you have done to date. Be sure that all who are participating at this point understand what a high-performance organization is. Review the environmental scan and stakeholder analysis and revise it based on their involvement. Be sure that your new allies have an opportunity to participate in defining the purpose, detailing the environment for change, identifying stakeholders, and spreading the word. In this way, you will be both educating a larger group and building their commitment to the change effort.

As you work to spread the word, use your steering group to help identify examples of organizations like yours that have taken significant steps toward high performance. Although the process used in these other efforts may not directly parallel yours, these examples can reassure people that this type of change can be made constructively.

At this point, you may begin to see some real disagreement surface. The disagreement may come from within the organization or from an outside interest; it may take the form of active lobbying against the initiative by a formidable outside group. Or you may be plagued by more passive non-concern expressed by an unwillingness to entertain changes in policies or practices within the organization.

It may be necessary to make some accommodations to disagreeing parties early in the process to avoid its premature death. Strategies you might employ include attempting to understand the cause of any resistance you are meeting and working to allay fears with examples of successful change. Or you may be able to defuse opponents by enlisting them in the design of the change process itself.

More radical strategies for addressing external resistance to change include a public information campaign to counter the resistance. If the problem is internal, you may appeal to higher-level authorities for support. These strategies carry with them significant risks, however, and should be considered as last resorts.

3. *Engage key players.* Your initial design team or steering group can help you develop a strategy to influence and engage a broader range of people, particularly those with power within your organization and, among outsiders, those who control its resources.

These key players should be approached individually and asked for help for two reasons. First, you will need their help if you are to make the kind of changes you are envisioning. Second, you will save time by involving them earlier rather than later in the change process. Anyone involved in and committed to a change effort will want to see their mark on it. Negotiating these points of view from the start will make the process more viable, increase commitment to the change effort, and save time in the long run.

For example, if you are in the city manager's office or the governor's office or are a department head, you may wish to begin educating and influencing the budget director or a key person in the budget office. Elected officials or other key staff members may also be interested in these ideas.

If you are a staff member in an agency without direct access to the director, you may approach other staff who are influential with those in leadership. You may also begin conversations with key legislators and staff, union leaders, and influential members of the private sector. These contacts, however, should be coordinated with elected or appointed leadership so that it does not appear that you are back-channeling.

If you are a manager or employee, now is the time to advise the key leaders of your interest and see if you can gain their support and commitment. If you can show how your planned effort fits in with the overall objectives of the political leaders, you will improve your chances of getting their support. If you can get the political leaders to adopt the effort as their own, be prepared to cede credit in exchange for progress.

If, however, you are a political leader, your job will be to convince those who have to carry out the changes you envision that these changes are in their best interest. You must be prepared to actively involve them in the planning process if you hope to have them adopt the changes and carry them on after you have gone.

Ultimately, building commitment to a change to a high-performance organization requires that a large number of people recognize the barriers to change as well as the opportunities. It requires facing squarely certain questions:

- Do we want to do this badly enough to deal with the delays, long hours, lack of budget, and resistance we are bound to encounter?
- Is the cost of staying the same greater than the cost of changing?
- What are the consequences of change for those in key power positions relating to the organization?

By this point, you have developed a cadre of people who have answered these questions and decided to proceed. This process of building commitment to change will continue and, if your efforts succeed, commitment to change will become a part of the culture of your organization.

With a clarified purpose, an environmental scan, a stakeholder analysis, and the first steps of building commitment for change complete, you are now ready to proceed. To this point, you have been working on an informal or ad hoc basis. We advise two main options for your next steps:

1. Begin to define more carefully the organization's vision, mission, and values.

2. Complete a more detailed organizational assessment of your present situation.

Both are critical elements of your change to high performance. Some people have chosen to do one first and then the other. Others use different groups and do them simultaneously. Familiarize yourself with the material in Chapters Five and Six in order to clarify what is involved in each; then choose the path that would work best in your situation.

# CHAPTER FIVE

# Crafting Your Vision, Mission, and Values

I n the public sector, a clear vision, a carefully crafted mission, and a set of values are crucial to creating a high-performance organization. They guide both the strategic direction of the agency and shape day-to-day decisions about what the organization does and how it does it.

Vision, mission, and values focus the energy of the organization on a common goal. They function much like a winged keel on the super-fast America's Cup sailing ships. The winged keel makes it possible for the ship to move into the wind. Without the winged keel extending down into the water, the boat would slip sideways rather than move forward across the water, as the sails capture the energy of the wind.

Organizations without a clear vision of the future or a solidly de-fined mission face a significant barrier to reaching their full perfor-mance potential. Energy is lost because they lack a clear guiding purpose. Both strategic and day-to-day decisions are made without an eye to the synergy necessary to make real progress on the organization's goals. Or worse, each part of the organization focuses solely on its im-mediate tasks. Worse yet, the parts may work at cross-purposes with one another.

During the early life of an organization, a single entrepreneur can drive the vision and mission. But as the organization matures, a broader process of engagement is necessary. Particularly in government, which is charged with undertaking the public purpose, the public and external stakeholders should participate.

The key to developing vision, mission, and values statements that work for your organization is to actively engage the people with a stake in the organization. You are probably familiar with war stories about mission-setting processes having gone awry. Maybe top management developed and imposed a mission or vision statement with little engagement of stakeholders. Or perhaps development was left to the planning staff, who arrived at an artfully worded document that few others in the organization care—or even know—about.

If that is true in your organization, you have much to overcome. You may well have to begin from scratch while facing the challenge of engaging key groups who are resentful of how they were treated in the past. In the end, the people in the organization and its other stakeholders are the critical factors. They must feel that the vision, mission, and value statements are theirs or are something to which they can be committed.

As you proceeded through the steps outlined in Chapter Four, you probably reached some tentative conclusions about the direction you want to move in. As the stakeholder analysis and environmental scan no doubt revealed, it is difficult to define these three crucial elements (vision, mission, and values) in the public sector. It is difficult in part because many different people with differing interests would like to set them for you. As you broaden your network of involvement, you encounter more diverse interests. Your job now is to focus these diverse interests on working toward common goals.

Sorting out the definitions of vision, mission, and values will be one of the first challenges you confront. Before you begin developing these concepts for your organization, take the time to clarify the differences within your working group so that everyone is familiar with the terms and what they mean.

The next steps entail developing statements of vision, mission, and values for your organization. You can take several approaches; these will be discussed in the section to follow. The options vary and are based on the extensiveness and public nature of the process.

As you do so, you also need to put in place a process for continuous review and improvement of your vision, mission, and values. They must be updated so that your organization can adapt to changing demands in the environment and changing needs within the organization.

## CLARIFYING OUR TERMS:
## VISION, MISSION, AND VALUES

A *vision statement* is a clear, concise description of what your organization is in business for—what you are trying to do. Its purpose is to communicate to all the stakeholders, especially employees, allies, and customers, just what the organization is about. Employees should be able to directly link their work to realizing the organization's overall vision.

In recent years, many governments have used public visioning processes to define results that stakeholders and the general public want them to achieve. States such as Oregon and Minnesota and many local governments used a variety of methods to gain extensive public input. Other organizations developed vision, mission, and value statements internally.

Many people are confused by the terms *vision* and *mission* and how they relate to statements of values. We provide you with some working definitions.

### Vision Statement

A *vision statement* describes a preferred future that spells out the conditions and quality of life that people with an interest in the organization want to achieve. Your vision statement should be focused on what will happen in the world if you are successful. It is *not* used to describe what your organization will look like. Two examples of vision statements follow.

> Minnesota will be a community of people who respect and care for one another. Our economic activity will create wealth and provide a good standard of living for all our people. Our citizens will be good thinkers, creative, always learning, with the skills to compete internationally. We will protect and enjoy the natural world. Our government will be responsive, effective, and close to the people.

> Twenty-first century Tennessee will have a literate citizenry of lifelong learners prospering in multicultural harmony, respectful of the environment, actively participating in the community, with healthy families, and economic security for all.

## Mission Statement

A *mission statement* answers the question: Why does the organization exist? A mission statement also outlines what the organization (working with others) plans to accomplish. Organizations have a larger sense of purpose that transcends providing for the needs of constituents and employees. They seek to contribute to the world in some unique way. To clarify this purpose, many organizations create mission statements. Two examples follow:

> The Fulton County Medical Center is a regional health service center working cooperatively with the community and other health care providers to meet the health care needs of the community by providing access to quality health care to the area's population.

> The mission of the Center for Families is to help parents provide the support, discipline, love, and encouragement their children need to become healthy and productive citizens. To accomplish this mission, the Center sponsors and cooperates in programs to improve the education, health, economic circumstances, and functioning of county families.

## Statement of Values

In addition to vision and mission statements, most high-performance organizations find it helpful to develop a *statement of values,* that is, to identify how they want the organization and its employees to act, consistent with its mission, along the path toward achieving its vision.

These are usually called the values of an organization. They might include such attributes as integrity, honesty, openness, freedom, collaboration, competition, equal opportunity, leanness, responsiveness, merit, or loyalty.

If you value teamwork, for example, but design a reward system that stresses individual performance, you have violated your values and must redesign. If your organization emphasizes courtesy and responsiveness, yet allows citizens to wait more than a month to receive services, you must redesign.

It is easier to list core values than to consistently live by them, but it is important to be clear about the organization's values. By doing so, you describe how the organization is committed to operate on a day-to-day basis while pursuing its vision. If you can establish the values by which your organization must run if it is to be successful, you will have criteria against which you can test alternate designs (see Exhibit 5.1).

| | |
|---|---|
| Self-direction | Openness |
| Respect of differences | Initiative |
| Growth and development | Fun |
| Flexibility | Integrity |
| Informed participation | Simplicity |
| Big-picture focus | Creativity |
| Customer first | Self-examination |
| Prudent risk taking | Trust |

Exhibit 5.1.    Examples of High-Performance Organization Values.

# DEVELOPING YOUR VISION, MISSION, AND VALUES

Public sector organizations have experimented with various ways to develop visions, missions, and value statements. The three processes that have emerged include

1. Engaging in a broad public visioning process

2. Developing vision, mission, or value statements internally

3. Letting a vision emerge from measurable goals or benchmarks

## Engaging in a Broad Public Visioning Process

Broad public visioning processes yield ideas and information critical to focusing your organization's strategic direction. They can also help build a solid foundation of support for your change plans. Broad public visioning processes, combined with measurable goals, can cut through the fog of uncertainty that often surrounds the purpose of public organizations.

Broad public visioning processes increase the visibility of the organization, and they signal its interest in engaging the public in setting a course for the future. If organizational credibility is at a low, if major change is contemplated that will require approval from outside stakeholders, or if you are interested in testing the political waters of alternative approaches, you may benefit from processes such as these (see Exhibit 5.2).

Launching a public visioning process may be easier if you are an elected or appointed official. Public involvement is, after all, a basic

*Support the Effort:* Doing this job right takes a real commitment of time, energy, and leadership from across the organization. Duncan Wyse, former director of the Oregon Progress Board, emphasizes that it takes more time and dedicated staff resources than most people expect. Limited staffing and an inability to engage top leadership directly in the visioning processes are a common Achilles heel.

*Start with a Framework:* Public input can be better focused when you have already developed a framework that begins to identify key issues, opportunities, and challenges.

*Test Consensus and Generate Feedback:* Oregon harnessed technology to accomplish this task. They used a simple personal-computer-based system. To test opinions or define where consensus might be on key issues, participants in town hall meetings and working groups voted electronically. The software reported back almost instantaneously how the group voted.

*Rely on Effective Facilitators:* Experienced facilitators are critical to the success of a broad visioning process. Facilitators can help the participants understand the goals and methods of a visioning process. They can also help the participants focus on key issues and better understand each other.

**Exhibit 5.2.    Some Tips for Conducting
a Broad Public Visioning Process.**

responsibility for those holding political office. But people at other levels within an organization can often garner the commitment of elected and appointed leadership to do so as well. This process would be enhanced if your other stakeholders included influential private sector representatives.

A process of this type would involve the public through town meetings, polls, focus groups, or other outreach efforts to bring new purpose to your organization while increasing the political credibility of the change process.

These processes will require a great deal of effort and may take many months to complete. They make the most sense for large organizations covering substantial geographical areas. States, counties, or cities as a whole might engage in broad public visioning processes, but individual agencies may want to take more manageable steps.

Oregon, Minnesota, and Texas provide concrete examples of public-visioning and goal-setting processes. The Oregon example, in particular, shows one approach to transforming a public visioning process into a driving force for more effective actions and investments at the state level.

In 1987, Oregon's Governor Neil Goldschmidt committed his administration to "creating a statewide capacity for long-term, well-managed growth while also making the state more competitive in the expanding global economy" (Oregon Economic Development Department, 1989, p. i). Simply coping with change can be an enormous challenge. But Oregon's leaders wanted to accomplish even more. They wanted to shape that future. To do so, the governor named a broad-based, public-private task force and challenged them to engage a wide array of stakeholders in shaping a comprehensive strategy for the state. In 1989, Governor Goldschmidt released *Oregon Shines,* a report championing a strategic vision that included specific priorities to concentrate attention. The strategic plan proposed that, through the collective efforts of government, business, and citizen groups, Oregon over the next two decades could achieve sustained economic prosperity, enhance its already high quality of life, maintain its natural environment, and build communities on a human scale.

## Developing Statements Internally

Your organization may have already developed vision and mission statements. In this case, your job will be to review these statements in concert with key stakeholders and suggest revisions to them if needed. Involving employees, customers, and other stakeholders in reviewing and validating these statements will help to acquaint your working group with these documents and reinvest them in working to achieve the vision set forth in them.

Internally developed statements can be generated through meetings with your steering or working group in which you answer the questions: Who are we? What do we do? For whom do we do it? How do we do it? and Why do we do it? From the answers to these questions, your group can prepare draft statements, share them with larger groups, including policymakers, and revise the statements with the goal of broadening support for your efforts.

Another way to internally develop your vision, mission, and value statements is through a technique called a "future search conference." In this approach, stakeholders are brought together for a one- or two-day session. They discuss the forces affecting the organization, its history, its successes and failures, and its hopes for the future. Through a series of large- and small-group exercises, they develop a vision for their organization.

Arlington, Virginia, developed guiding principles through an internal visioning process (Parkhurst, 1994). For several years, county staff worked on formulating "principles of government service." These six values, or principles, were developed by a team of managers and employees and promulgated for the organization. They form the basis for their organizational and services-related improvement efforts. Arlington worked with the Center for Public Service from the University of Virginia on a model that focuses on vision, mission, and values. They started by trying to figure out what they needed for the next decade. This led them to develop the list of six principles: high-quality services, commitment to employees, diversity, teamwork, leadership, and empowerment. They assembled an implementation team, and each department developed an implementation plan for the principles. These plans are highly varied in terms of their approach. Each organizational unit has some group working on them. One has a board of employees; others have management groups.

## Letting a Vision Emerge from Measurable Goals

Some organizations allow a vision of the future to emerge from work on measurable goals and the mission of the organization. This technique can be used successfully only if the measurable goals and mission of the organization result in a coherent vision of the future for the organization and its affected environment.

Iowa developed a visioning and benchmarking process that allows the vision to emerge from specific, measurable goals. Begun as a focus on investment decision making, the state has conducted a broad-based process to set measurable goals. From these goals, the state crafted its vision of the future. The vision will guide some of the state's investment decisions.

Our reconnaissance of high-performance initiatives in the public sector found unanimity on the importance of a clear mission and vision for change that is not limited to a two- or four-year term of office. Participants and leaders of these change processes also stressed that vision, mission, and value statements were most useful in motivating employees. They help inform other stakeholders about the purposes of the organizational changes. In high-performing organizations, each employee understands the organization's vision and mission, as well as their individual mission within that context. They also have signed up to operate on a day-to-day basis in a manner that reflects the organization's values.

In moving through the process of defining your vision, mission, and values, your steering group should be responsible for communicating the need to define the vision, mission, and values, for developing proposed statements, and for managing a process for their adoption. Experience suggests that these processes can easily become bogged down in definitional disputes over the differences between vision, mission, and value statements. We suggest that you not spend too much time on debates of this nature. It is important to reach enough agreement to proceed. You need not develop the perfect vision statement.

## CONTINUOUS IMPROVEMENT OF VISION, MISSION, AND VALUES

Because of the impact of the larger environment on our organizations, the development of vision, mission, and value statements should be part of a process of continuous improvement.

As the environment changes, our organization must reassess its direction and purpose. Recall the story of the slide-rule makers who believed that their mission was to make slide-rules versus the slide-rule makers who believed that their mission was to make scientific instruments. It is clear which of these companies is still in business.

If vision, mission, and values statements are too narrowly defined, they are more likely to become SPLOTS—strategic plans languishing on the shelf. Rather, they must be living, vital components of high-performance organizations, used as standards for judging performance and progress. (See Chapter Seven for a discussion of setting performance measures and crafting accountability systems.)

To ensure that the crafting of vision, mission, and value statements is not a one-time exercise, you might consider conducting periodic audits. With an audit, you reassess the performance of your organization against your vision, mission, and values, which must also be subject to review with changes in political leadership. For political leaders to recognize the utility of this process, particularly if it was initiated prior to their tenure, the leader must be able to see the outcomes for the organization or jurisdiction itself. But they should also be able to help redirect the organization's mission and values to accommodate their priorities.

Periodic review of vision, mission, and values not only shows you where progress is being made but also where change can or should be made.

Building a process to continuously revisit and improve your vision, mission, and values will help you move through the process more quickly. If those participating think they must get it absolutely right the first time around, then the process may seem interminable. If, however, those participating realize that this is the first cut that will be revisited and improved over time, they will be more willing to move on to subsequent steps of the process (see Exhibit 5.3).

| What to Do | How to Do It |
|---|---|
| Develop and communicate a clear image of the future | 1. Develop the vision and values for the future |
| | 2. Develop as complete a picture of the future as possible |
| | 3. Communicate repeatedly—tell and sell |
| | 4. Describe how things will operate in the future—paint scenarios |
| | 5. Use multiple media |
| Demonstrate leadership support | 1. Model the behavior; be consistent |
| | 2. Provide resources |
| | 3. Use "hallway conversations" and other informal means of communication |
| | 4. Visibly demonstrate harmony among the leadership |
| Create an identity for the change and the level of support | 1. Use symbolic acts |
| | 2. Create effective names and words to describe the change process |
| | 3. Use graphics |
| | 4. Articulate metaphors |

Exhibit 5.3.    Creating the Vision.

# CHAPTER SIX

# Conducting Useful Organizational Assessments

A ssessment entails making quantitative and qualitative judgments about how well an organization is achieving its vision and mission and whether it is doing so based on its values. Assessment is about objective measurement. But it is also leavened by a healthy dose of intuition and judgment. Ultimately, assessment is done to influence behavior, both internally and externally, in any organization.

## WHY SHOULD YOU ASSESS?

You may shy away from assessment for a variety of reasons. This often happens in the public sector because people fear how the results will be used. Staff and management alike will argue over the assessment tools, the assessment procedures, the need for assessment, and how the results are to be interpreted. In the worst case, types of data, their availability, and their inherent weaknesses will be bandied about until your mind dulls and your eyes glaze over. Behind these responses to assessment is the fear that those being assessed will not measure up in some way. Also, people in the public sector have seen data misused and manipulated for all types of purposes.

Do not get mired in these responses to assessment and lose sight of what you are trying to assess and why. To move through this resistance, keep in mind and clearly articulate the reasons why you should assess your organization. Assessment serves three main purposes. It can

1. Motivate us to change
2. Help us select targets of opportunity
3. Monitor progress

The first purpose is frequently overlooked. The second is often given too much weight. And the third is too rarely done. The following sections provide more information about the purposes for doing an assessment and methods of conducting each type.

## Assessment to Motivate Change

At the early stages of your effort, you should focus on collecting and presenting data that will illustrate the need for change. You will want to document this need and to make the case for change. We are much more likely to be influenced by vivid and salient data that are clearly presented. In general, person-to-person communication is more motivating than statistical information, unless the statistics are graphically presented and overwhelmingly clear. In addition, people are much more motivated by data they collect themselves than those they read about.

Two methods of assessment are particularly effective in motivating change: *voice-of-the-customer assessments* and *benchmarking.* These methods can also be used for other purposes; both are discussed in more detail later in this chapter. Also, both methods can yield information that can help establish the need for change and motivate others to move toward high performance.

## Assessment for Selecting Targets of Opportunity

Assessing your organization will reveal some areas where performance is high and others where improvement is needed. Because the assessment is part of your effort to move toward high performance, it is a time when you are giving form to what you believe is critical. You are deciding what is important to measure. Several approaches are used, including using quality-related criteria, value statements, and components of organizational design. These three approaches are discussed later in this chapter.

### Assessment for Monitoring Progress

A private sector leader once summed up the value of measuring things by saying, "What is measured gets done; what is rewarded gets done well." Measuring something brings attention to it. Knowing what kind of data to provide to whom is part of the art of assessment.

If the vision, mission, and values of the organization have been spelled out before the assessment begins, and if progress has been made toward making the goals of the organizations measurable, assessing progress will mean choosing a few quantitative and qualitative indicators of organizational performance and then charting them.

As an assessment, these indicators can be examined in the past tense. When assessing the performance of a job training agency, one might ask, How many job placements resulted in people staying on the job for over a year? Another question might be, Has this percentage been growing over the past five years? For the future, the same yardstick might be applied as the organization changes. Ask this question: Are our changes resulting in an increase in the placement rate for longlasting jobs? If not, perhaps the redesign is not working, or other areas need attention.

## TYPES OF ASSESSMENTS

High-performance organizations continually assess their performance and learn from those assessments. Assessment is a source of information. It is not a way to play "gotcha." To move in this direction, you will need to put a solid measurement system in place.

Ultimately, a high-performance organization needs a measurement system that operates at several levels and is capable of linking the performance of groups of employees to the performance of the enterprise. In designing any type of measurement tool, you may want to review the characteristics of a good measurement system. They include the following:

*Completeness:* Do the indicators adequately reflect the overall objective? For example, return on investment is a good measure of income but not of equity. Similarly, quality, accuracy, and timeliness may be useful in some circumstances.

*Timeliness:* Can the measurement be taken soon after the need to measure rather than being held to an arbitrary date or performed as an "autopsy," such as an exit interview or a returned product. In general, the measures should be robust enough to identify a problem in a timely fashion, not only at the annual performance review.

*Visibility:* Can the measure be openly tracked by those being measured? If the system is not transparent, no one can see what performance is being tracked. Lack of transparency or visibility can doom a measurement system.

*Cost:* It may always be less expensive to use data already being collected for some other purposes. An employee survey is costly to perform three times a year. However, a survey attached to another document may be less costly.

*Interpretability:* The measure should be easy to understand, and the data should be comparable across your organization and with other organizations. If one manager interprets a measure one way and another a different way, then the measure is probably too subjective.

*Importance:* Does the measure clearly connect to important business objectives? Although quality, timeliness, and accuracy may seem important, they ignore other factors and can lead to a counting exercise.

*Time balance:* The measurement system should reflect a balance between long- and short-term objectives. Meeting short-term objectives at the expense of long-term objectives pushes the problem further down the line.

*Motivational balance:* The overall measurement system must also find a balance between competitive invigoration and collaborative teamwork.

To be effective, the purposes of the measurement system must be known and understood throughout the organization. If the purpose is not well communicated, the definitional errors will look like problems associated with the measurement system itself. No amount of tweaking the measurement system can rectify problems attributed to a lack of performance definition.

Keeping in mind the different reasons for assessing your organization, you may want to review the different types of assessment that seem to be particularly useful in helping organizations move toward higher performance. These include assessment of the

- Current organizational culture and structure
- Satisfaction of your customers
- Satisfaction of your employees
- Need for change

## Assessing Organizational Culture and Structure

In literature exhorting private companies to redesign themselves or in descriptions of successful companies, much emphasis is placed on organizational culture. The culture embodies the rules with which an organization works. But it also reflects many intangibles such as teamwork, entrepreneurial spirit, innovative or creative thinking, and other valuable characteristics. In the private sector, the most successful companies seem to have developed and maintained an environment in which these characteristics flourish.

Part of their success lies in crafting reward systems within their organizations. If innovation is valued, top managers are likely to express the sentiment, "In our company, it's OK to make a mistake." Innovators make mistakes. But they try again. In reshaping the organizational culture, successful change agents imbue the work environment with the values that they profess.

To assess the organizational culture in the public sector, you will compare the statement of values guiding the organization against how people work, both individually and collectively. If telling the truth is a value, then agency employees must be willing to say to a customer or a community group, "Yes, we made a mistake." If acting in a professional manner is a value for a school, then teachers must be willing to work late to return calls to parents.

Other organizational design features contribute to the culture and should be kept in mind as you craft your assessment. For example, if there is a steep hierarchy with lots of perks at the top, this gives a clear message about who is valued in the organization.

A close look at the rewards or penalties for employees must also accompany an examination of the organizational culture in the public sector. There should be a way to reward behavior conducive to improving the organizational culture. Making a list of rewards and penalties that apply in the day-to-day life of an organization can reveal barriers to improving the organizational culture (see additional discussion and a sample survey in Chapter Four).

Another way to assess the organizational culture is to ask employees, customers, vendors, and suppliers about it. Having worked in or with your organization for years, these people are likely to have a very good idea about how the organization operates at the ground level. Using focus groups, surveys, or individual interviews, it is possible to get a good assessment of how the organizational culture evolved.

## Assessing Customer Satisfaction

"The customer is always right" is a slogan often heard but not always followed in the private sector. Making customers happy enough to return and spend their money on your goods or services is one key to a high-performance organization in the private sector.

As usual, it is not so simple in the public sector. Sometimes, the customer is not right. A property owner may engage in a frivolous appeal of a tax assessment. But being wrong does not mean that the customer should be treated impolitely or in an unresponsive manner. Sometimes, the different customers of government have different points of view. Your job will be to try to find high-performing options for reconciling these points of view.

In Tampa, Florida, for example, an assessment of customer satisfaction motivated significant changes in the way the city delivers services to the poor and uninsured. In this case, the customers were those who turned to emergency rooms for health care and the taxpayers who saw the cost for indigent health care jump as much as 20 percent annually. Indigent patients seeking health care resorted to emergency services because of their lack of insurance coverage and inability to pay. Treatment was deferred until it reached crisis levels, compromising health and necessitating more expensive services. The solution was a managed care network to provide primary and preventative care for the uninsured. A one-half cent sales tax increase pays for the network. Emergency room use has fallen by 27 percent.

Many of the techniques for assessing customer satisfaction developed in the private sector can be used by public sector agencies. One of these techniques is the voice-of-the-customer assessment.

Voice-of-the-customer techniques were developed in the private sector during the TQM movement. These techniques are used to discover customers' needs and expectations. By using both survey and interview techniques, you make it easy for customers to express themselves, even to complain. The organization then uses this information to address the causes behind customer satisfaction or dissatisfaction.

Open-ended questions are frequently used when doing voice-of-the-customer assessments. An open-ended question allows the respondents greater latitude in answering questions. (Closed-ended questions usually can be answered with a simple yes or no or a single-word answer.) Open-ended questions begin with "How" or "Why." Closed-ended questions begin with "Is" or "Do." An open-ended question would be, What about our service satisfies you? A closed-ended question would be, Do you like our service?

The first question allows you to understand your customer and gives you information that you can use to improve your performance. The latter only tells you whether the customer is satisfied or not.

Voice-of-the-customer techniques are useful in the early stages of a change to high performance because they can help focus the organization on the need for change. They can help identify customers' needs, as they relate to the organization.

Examples from the private sector illustrate the application of this technique. The Quaker Oats Company frequently listens to the voices of their customers. They know that a majority of their customers are mothers. By talking to these mothers, they discovered that many of them work but still want to provide their children with a hot breakfast in the morning. Listening to their customers' voices led the company to develop microwaveable oatmeal, which comes in single-serving containers. That way, busy mothers can pop the container into the microwave and quickly prepare a hot breakfast for their children. Quaker Oats never would have discovered this product if they had just asked, Do you like our oatmeal?

In a large teaching hospital, the senior administrative staff used voice-of-the-customer techniques to identify what its various constituents wanted. After brainstorming a list of key customers and identifying some critical questions, the group divided the list and conducted the interviews. The CEO thought the assessment was particularly effective. His staff heard firsthand some of the problems he had been sharing with them. Only this time they were moved by the comments. They finally saw in more concrete terms what he was talking about.

## Assessing Employee Satisfaction

As part of the assessment of the organizational culture, you will have set in motion a number of collaborative efforts among employees. Building on these contacts, you should also use a variety of techniques to assess employee satisfaction. These techniques can be similar to those you use for assessing customer satisfaction. They should be varied and open-ended where possible.

In a large organization, it may be necessary to use surveys, focus groups, and other sampling techniques to assess the job satisfaction of differing groups of employees. Basic data, such as turnover rates, should also be marshaled for this assessment.

Public sector union organizations can be a strong ally in completing this part of the assessment of employee satisfaction. Because you will have included a union representative on your steering group, that person could become a natural leader in the employee satisfaction assessment (see Exhibit 6.1).

In general, if your employees are not happy, they will not be performing according to the values set forth by the organization. Nor will they be accomplishing the mission. If they are fulfilling the mission and are still dissatisfied, then something may be wrong with the mission itself. Open yourself to criticism from employees as well as customers. From these can develop many positive changes for your organization.

## Assessing the Need for Change

Thus far in the assessment process, you have stayed pretty close to home—examining your customers, organizational culture, and employee satisfaction. To assess the need for change, you can also look outside your immediate stakeholders at similar organizations and how well they operate. Several techniques can be used for accomplishing this task, including

- Benchmarking and best practices
- Quality-related criteria
- Components of organizational design

BENCHMARKING AND BEST-PRACTICES ASSESSMENTS. Benchmarking and the less rigorous best-practices assessments are both techniques

---

Some of the questions you might ask employees include:

- What do you like about your job?
- What do you dislike?
- What is the relationship between your job and the overall mission of the organization?
- Do you feel that you have enough latitude to make decisions?
- Has your training prepared you well enough for a broad range of assignments?
- What barriers to your effectiveness are created by this organization?
- What should people be rewarded for doing in this organization?

Exhibit 6.1.    Sample Employee Satisfaction Questions.

that can help instigate action. Benchmarking can be used to identify the best enterprise in a particular process and to compare yourself against its standards of performance. This is the private sector's use of the term. It should not be confused with another type of benchmarking used in the public sector, which is a goal-setting exercise. Benchmarking as it relates to goal setting is discussed in detail in Chapter Seven.

Benchmarking against best practices was a critical element of Xerox's initial change effort. General Electric modified the notion of benchmarking and called their process *best practices.* Best-practices techniques identify what the best practices or effective ideas are worldwide.

Steps distilled from private sector experience may help you benchmark the performance of your organization with another organization.

*Step 1: Identify target.* To benchmark or conduct a best-practices study, you must identify what you want to benchmark. Is it your distribution process, your collection process, or your service delivery process?

*Step 2: Document current efforts.* Once you have identified what you want to do, you need to identify how you're doing. Questions you need to address include, What does your process look like? What do you want your system to do? How is your department structured? Find comparable performance data from across the organizations. How long does it take to service a claim, or how many complaints can you respond to in a day?

*Step 3: Identify best example.* After you understand what you want to do and how you are currently doing, the next step is to identify the best organization in that area. For example, if you are interested in a local process to create high performance, you might want to look at another community that has earned a reputation or awards for performance.

Another way to identify high-performance organizations is to ask experts in the field. Colleagues in other places, membership associations, and consultants found on your list of contacts are almost always good sources for identifying benchmark companies or public sector organizations. You can also ask academics, government experts, or award-winning units. But in any case, ask more than one contact.

Many leading-edge organizations, including those in the public sector, are reluctant to spend the time it takes to have you benchmark them unless there is something in it for them. There are a number of ways to make this a valuable experience for all participants. Some, like the Saturn Corporation, schedule tours but charge a fee. Others will allow only customers or suppliers access to their information. It may also be possible to obtain access to information by offering to provide the participants with the results of the study. In this case, the benchmarked organization may gain a new perspective through your work and may be partially compensated for taking the time to help you study their work.

*Step 4: Specify data needs and collection methods; collect data.* Once you have pinpointed the best organization, you will need to decide what kind of data you will collect and how they will be collected. Will you visit the enterprise, or will you do a phone or mail survey? To determine what information you will collect, refer back to your decisions about the benchmark targets (that is, what you want to know about the organization in order to improve your organization).

*Step 5: Analyze data.* Collecting the data is the fun part. Analyzing the data is hard work. Questions you will want to ask are: Are they doing better than we are? Why are they better? What can we learn from them? How can we apply what we have learned to our enterprise?

Benchmarking and best-practices studies are expensive. To gain a return on your investment, it is critical not to end the process with data collection but to take the ideas and incorporate them into your plans. To help with this, some organizations have found that site visits are a good tool to reinforce the ideas gathered in a benchmarking or best-practices study and to help them think through the process in implementation.

A midwestern agency used benchmarking as a way to gather data for restructuring their accounting services. A design team working on the project analyzed their own accounting process and then, with the help of a consultant, identified some state-of-the art accounting services. The team split up into subteams, and each visited some of their identified benchmarked organizations. When they came back together, they compiled their information and compared what they had found.

When the Federal Aviation Administration (FAA) was developing a new high-involvement air traffic control unit, the entire design team took a trip to the Saturn plant in Tennessee. Seeing what a high-performance plant looked like helped them crystallize in their minds what they wanted to create and made it possible for them to decide what they had to do.

QUALITY-RELATED CRITERIA. Some agencies use modified Baldrige Award scoring methods to conduct their assessments. Baldrige criteria are designed to help companies enhance their competitiveness through a focus on results-oriented goals, the delivery of ever-improving value to customers, improved marketplace performance, and improvement of overall company operational performance.

The award criteria include leadership, information and analysis, strategic quality planning, human resource development and management, management of process quality, quality and operational results, and customer focus and satisfaction. This type of assessment highlights areas you will want to return to as you plan your change.

Using quality-related criteria can be a valuable part of assessing the need for change in your organization. Keep in mind, however, that the primary focus is on your mission and how adhering to these criteria can help contribute to it, not on the criteria themselves.

COMPONENTS OF ORGANIZATIONAL DESIGN. High-performance organizations are deliberately designed to be high performing. Organizational design involves aligning the features of an organization (task or technology, people, structure, human resource systems, organizational values and norms, and information-decision systems) with its strategy (the functions the organization will perform, the products or services it will produce, and the markets it will serve and those external elements affecting the organization's ability to implement its strategy, including suppliers, customers, competitors and regulators) in order to produce desired results (Galbraith and Lawler, 1995). Setting your targets of opportunity based on this "fit" model is well known and widely used.

If you look at your current organization, its design can be a result of longstanding personnel policies, budgeting processes, collective bargaining agreements, cultural norms, or informal agreements, and it can reflect the values of the organization. These design elements lock in organizational functioning and make it hard to improve performance through simple or limited changes (see Exhibit 6.2).

Any number of data-gathering methodologies can be used to gather responses to these questions. Organizations have conducted surveys comparing responses from various different levels of the organization. Others have conducted focus groups. Still others have pulled together large groups of employees in a conference to respond to the questions in small work groups and then share their responses. You may want to use a combination of these methods. The questions are meant to be guidelines.

This chapter has given you a sense of the reasons for assessing your organization and some idea of the types of assessments that you might

*Inputs*

1. Strategy

   Is there a well-defined strategy that provides sufficient direction for the design process?

   Is the strategy well known, understood, and believed throughout the organization?

2. Task Environment

   What changing aspects of the environment have implications for how the organization is designed?

   Is the organization sufficiently flexible to respond to the rate of change and the complexity in its environment?

*Design Components*

1. Task-Technology

   Are the tools and processes suitable for effective task performance?

   Does the physical layout of the workplace support task accomplishment and coordination?

   Are jobs designed to be motivating?

   Is work designed so that people can easily work out interdependencies and process uncertainties?

2. People

   Do people have the technical, professional, and interpersonal skills to do their jobs effectively?

   Do the jobs meet the needs and preferences of the employees?

3. Information-Decision Systems

   Is information that permits good decision making collected and shared? In a timely manner?

   Are decisions being made at the location in the organization that has the best information to make the decision?

4. Human Resource Systems

   Do the human resources management or personnel practices select, develop, and reward people for the kinds of performance needed to perform the organization's tasks?

5. Structure

   Do the groupings in the organization provide focus on the key variables in its environment?

   Does the structure facilitate the needed coordination and information flow?

6. Organizational Values and Norms

   What values and patterns of behavior prevalent in the organization work against the accomplishment of the performance values that have been established?

*Outputs*

1. Performance Outcomes

   Is the organization achieving its performance goals?

   What are the trends? Are they improving or deteriorating? Why?

2. Human Outcomes

   Is the organization achieving its human objectives?

   What are the trends?

**Exhibit 6.2.  Some Issues to Address in Assessing Organizational Design.**

employ, depending on your purpose. Remember that your organization will pay attention to what you assess and that the purposes and uses of your assessments must be clear and well understood.

The measurement system is like the instrument panel in an airplane. It should be designed to allow you to gauge how well the organization is performing and to navigate your move toward high performance. The results of your assessments will give you important information on the course to take as you develop your plan for change.

# CHAPTER SEVEN

# Designing a Results-Driven Plan for Change

I n Chapter Five, we explored the need to clarify the vision or preferred future of high-performance organizations, their reason for existing, and their values. In Chapter Six, we discussed how to set a baseline to help clarify your direction and your areas of focus for getting there. Understanding how to build a plan for change that is geared toward achieving your vision is the next step.

## BUILDING A FRAMEWORK FOR ACCOUNTABILITY

In high-performance organizations, accountability is the responsibility accepted by each person, both individually and as part of a team, to achieve results. That shared responsibility for results is the glue that holds the organization together. It provides cause for celebration when targets are met. And it offers an opportunity to make course corrections when they are not met.

This is a relatively new idea in the public sector. Traditionally, government accountability has focused more on adherence to procedures. Procedures provide some assurances regarding the proper conduct of the public's business. For example, procedures are designed to reduce incidents of fraud and abuse. They enable the orderly and equitable distribution of funds. They help ensure that only those who are eligible for services receive them. But they are not an adequate substitute for results. Public servants may be following all of the procedures and still be unable to improve education, child health, or public safety.

What does it really mean to be results-driven? How does this shape your plan for change? A results-driven public organization begins with all parties understanding and sharing responsibility for achieving success. The first steps in building your plan for change include (1) quantifying your vision by translating it into specific, measurable, and achievable results and (2) developing the capacity to determine whether you have achieved them or not. This sets the foundation for an organization whose workforce is accountable for results.

The second steps involve (1) aligning your policies and programs, work processes, and culture to facilitate achieving the intended results. You should also (2) examine the array of organizational change strategies that have been taken elsewhere so you will have the benefit of experience to guide you. Think of these change strategies as tools to enable you to proceed. They are means, not ends, and they can be tailored to your organization and its environment.

The final set of steps reinforce learning and accountability for results by (1) building capacity to implement change and by (2) evaluating and communicating, and continuously improving your efforts.

## DESIGNING THE APPROACH INCLUSIVELY

As you begin, you need to create a planning structure. Some organizations hire outside experts to help design their change strategy. Others rely on champions from within. No matter where you find your experts, remember two important rules of human nature. First, the plan must be owned and operated by people within the organization who have the authority to make change. Those at the highest levels within both management and labor must give license and legitimacy to the plan. They must make the effort a priority, define its general purpose, and establish the broad principles to guide its implementation. And second, your best source of expertise comes from listening to people who are in the trenches doing the work each day.

Formalize and energize the process with a working group, a steering committee, or a design team. Call it what you like, but keep in mind that you will enrich the design and create more buy-in if you adhere to these simple principles:

- Managers and employees must be part of the working group.
- People with authority and ability to move mountains must be part of the working group.
- People with knowledge of the details and who can follow through should provide staff support to the effort.
- The authority of the working group must be clear. Its role and responsibilities must be understood by all of its members and by the full organization. Tasks, time lines, decision processes, and individual responsibilities must be clarified.

## DEFINING RESULTS: SETTING THE FOUNDATION FOR ACCOUNTABILITY

In the private sector, the elements that allow organizations to redesign themselves are often already in place. By and large, private sector organizations have a good idea about products or services they produce. They know how well their products are selling and whether they are making a profit.

In government, however, it is hard to develop analogous measurements. Government's products are sometimes less tangible. Its customers may be less obvious. And profit, loss, or return on investment is not easy to calculate. Nevertheless, it is critical that public sector organizations attempt to develop analogs to products and services, customer satisfaction, and profit or loss as part of their effort to define results.

For public sector organizations, we have already discussed the importance of engaging the organization and many of its stakeholders in a process that defines exactly what the organization should do.

To build an accountability system to support high performance, you will need to translate your vision into measurable results. Reaching agreement on results is tough in the public sector for several reasons. First, the conversation leading to agreement on any results that matter to the public deals with deeply held, and often conflicting, values. There are strong advocates on all sides.

Second, we have a long tradition in the public sector of creating a new program for every new problem. As a consequence, we now have an entangled landscape of overlapping programs with, at times, inconsistent goals and rules. Or we have programs operating at cross-purposes. Another consequence is that many public officials view the world through their program lens. They see programs less as a means toward an end and more as an end in themselves. This makes it hard to discuss the underlying purpose for which a program is designed or whether that purpose is being achieved.

Third, many of the results government is responsible for are elusive. They are often difficult to measure. It can be even more difficult to determine the underlying cause of success or failure. Many policymakers, program managers, and employees are reluctant to have decisions hinge on such imperfect proxies for cause and effect.

Finally, many public employees are uncomfortable with accountability for results. They worry that all this talk about results is merely shorthand for eliminating their jobs. They worry about being held accountable for things beyond their control. And they are concerned that they will have little say in the process.

Despite these difficulties, building this framework for accountability will help you judge whether or not you are successful. It will enable you to judge policies and programs by measuring their results against agreed-upon standards (Brizius and Campbell, 1991). As you begin to build this framework you should focus on these key questions:

- In the broadest sense, what would we want to observe to give us confidence that we are achieving our desired result? What would be different? What is our product?

- Different for whom? Who would and who would not benefit? Who is the customer?

- Of what we would like to observe, what can we realistically quantify? What is measurable?

- What are reasonable increments of time after which we should see measurable progress?

- What baseline can we establish to mark progress?

- What meaningful comparisons should we make to better understand progress? Increments of change from our baseline? Comparison to an established standard? Increments of change compared to similar populations in other locations? Increments of change from one to another point in time?

- What data are we currently gathering? How well do they measure the conditions or trends that matter most?

To answer these questions, however, we in the public sector must shift our focus dramatically, from measuring and rewarding the processes programs go through, to an emphasis on performance. In our schools, for example, it is no longer adequate to graduate young people based on the time they have spent in classes or meeting minimum standards. Instead, we will confer high school graduation on the basis of what students can do—read, write, compute, analyze, think, and work together—rather than on how long they have attended our schools. In workplace, family, and community literacy programs, we will measure how much progress students make along the literacy continuum and whether they are meeting their own goals for literacy instead of focusing on how many slots we have created or how many people we have served (see Exhibit 7.1).

How will we accomplish this shift from a process to a results orientation? We need to look more closely at developing measures linked directly to achieving your vision.

## Choosing Your Terms

Because this is an emerging field, people often use different terms to mean the same thing. For example, the term *results* has been used interchangeably with *outcomes, benchmarks, goals*, or *milestones*. People quibble over words like *output, indicators*, or *targets*. To avoid confusion, choose your terms, be sure that people understand what they mean, and be consistent. Remember, results are about ends, not means. They reflect an improved condition. They are quantifiable. They should specify what will change and for whom. Exhibit 7.2 offers one way to define terms. You will find a more complete glossary at the end of this chapter.

Keep focused on the task. You are developing a framework for accountability that will help you determine how well your organization is progressing toward achieving results. Develop a workable lexicon and try to minimize confusion.

## Establishing Measurable Results

In an earlier step, we reviewed steps needed to set the vision, mission, and values of our organizations. Now, we will establish clear and measurable results or outcomes to quantify the vision. Measurable results or outcomes will guide you on the path to achieving your vision and will tell you whether you are improving over time. Results

|  | Traditional | Results-Driven |
|---|---|---|
| Goal | Designed to minimize fraud, waste, and abuse<br><br>Designed to ensure equity and fairness<br><br>Designed to minimize incidence of poor judgment | Designed to ensure that the policy or program results in an improved condition and is done fairly, equitably, and honestly<br><br>Designed to empower people to use good judgment |
| Tools | Detailed regulation<br><br>Audit<br><br>Hearings and reviews | Memoranda of understanding<br><br>Performance agreements<br><br>Partnership agreements<br><br>Performance measurement |
| Process | Rules and special program requirements tightly prescribed:<br>• Reporting on program operations<br>• Allocating costs<br>• Procuring goods and services<br>• Planning program operations<br>• Determining and validating eligibility for narrow range of services | Clear and shared understanding of<br>• Results<br>• Definitions<br>• Funding and programs<br>• Performance indicators<br>Has flexibility to make decisions within broad parameters<br><br>Allows people to identify barriers and opportunities<br><br>Lets people eliminate barriers and act on opportunities<br><br>Permits continuous improvement |

Exhibit 7.1.   Accountability: Traditional and Emerging.

or outcomes should be stated in terms of specific future dates so that looking back, you will know whether you achieved them in the time frame you anticipated.

The results, or outcomes-setting, process attempts to quantify particular conditions and to track progress in improving these conditions over time. For instance, to track family economic well-being, you might use two different measures: (1) the number of families living in poverty and (2) the per capita income. To turn these measures into true outcomes, a target date for achieving a certain amount of improvement would be set. See Exhibit 7.3 for examples of population-wide results or outcomes.

*Result or Outcome Measures:* Reflect an improved condition or circumstance over time. Usually, these measures are reflected in aggregate demographic and economic data for the nation, a state, or region.

*Performance Measures:* Reflect the progress of a strategy toward achieving its intended results. Performance measures can apply to an initiative, a program, or group of related programs.

*Output Measures:* Reflect the volume of activity achieved by a strategy, initiative, or program—for example, the percentage of children immunized or the number of high school students completing structured work experience.

*Input Measures:* Reflect the level of effort involved in implementing a strategy, initiative, or program—for example, the number of students entering work experience programs or the number of health aides administering vaccines.

**Exhibit 7.2.   Definitions of Key Terms.**

*Result-Outcome 1:* By the year 2000, the percentage of families living in poverty will be reduced from the current rate of 13 percent to no more than 8 percent.

*Result-Outcome 2:* By the year 2000, the per capita income in the state will be 105 percent of the national average.

*Result-Outcome 3:* By the year 2000, the number of children abused or neglected per 1,000 children under the age of eighteen will decline from 12.3 to 6.

*Result-Outcome 4:* By the year 2000, the violent crime rate will be reduced from 10.1 per 100,000 people to 5.0.

**Exhibit 7.3.   Results-Outcomes Examples.**

Oregon is well along in a pioneering state and local effort—the Oregon Benchmarks—that focuses on results that matter to Oregonians. Through a participatory planning process that began in 1987, the citizens of Oregon established a long-range vision of a better place. The Oregon Progress Board, a bipartisan citizen body, was created by the legislature to translate this vision into a set of targets (the benchmarks) and measurable indicators. The board keeps track of achievement toward the benchmarks and reports this to the legislature and the public every two years.

The Oregon Benchmarks cover issues as wideranging as ecosystem protection, urban mobility, and industrial diversification. Human investment benchmarks focus on such outcomes as reduced pregnancy among teens, diminished crime and recidivism, lower unemployment, higher per capita income, greater early childhood immunization, and stronger K–12 student achievement. The important characteristics of measurable results or outcomes are that they be

- Measurable: We can find out whether they were achieved.
- Dated: They have a time goal.
- Relevant: They matter to the customer, or the public wants them.

To help you in the process of developing your own results or outcomes, we have included samples from Oregon and Minnesota in Exhibit 7.4.

### Defining Performance Measures

Although results or outcomes specify the desired conditions to be achieved in the future, they do not specify how these conditions will be achieved or the extent to which this will be accomplished through public programs. In most instances, government action can only produce a portion of the change needed to achieve a result. Other factors, such as changing conditions in a global economy, will also have a significant impact.

|  | 1980 | 1995 | 2000 | 2010 |
|---|---|---|---|---|
| *Oregon Benchmarks* | | | | |
| *Equal Opportunity, Social Harmony, and Economic Participation* | | | | |
| Income per capita as a percentage of Oregon median among . . . | | | | |
| African Americans | 68.4 | 75 | 80 | 90 |
| American Indians | 63.2 | 75 | 80 | 90 |
| Asians | 75.2 | 75 | 80 | 90 |
| Hispanics | 58.3 | 75 | 80 | 90 |
| *Minnesota Milestones* | | | | |
| Percentage of people who have been crime victims | 54.9 | 45 | 40 | 35 |
| Infant mortality rate (%) | 10 | 6.5 | 5.0 | 4.5 |
| Number of public access sites on lakes and rivers | NA | 2,300 | 2,500 | 2,800 |

Exhibit 7.4.    Sample Benchmarks from Oregon and Minnesota.

A second foundation activity for design change, therefore, will be for you to quantify, where possible, what your organization or its components have to achieve to contribute to achieving the result. This will involve estimating how many people must be helped through policies or other actions taken during the next five, ten, and twenty years to achieve results and identifying quantitative and qualitative performance measures for each action. A performance measure is the desired result of an action or a coordinated set of actions by government aimed at achieving a specific result. Achieving a result or outcome may require achieving several different performance measures.

As you begin the process of developing your performance measures, remember that they should be stated in quantifiable terms and be linked directly to the achievement of a result or outcome. Examples of performance measures follow.

> Over three years, the number of non-English speaking recent immigrants who can speak, write, and read English well enough to become employed will increase by fifty-four thousand. (Linked to Result-Outcome #1)

> Employees in at least half of the businesses in the state will increase productivity so that average wages improve to at least $10 per hour during the next two years. (Linked to Result-Outcome #2)

> By the year 2000, the number of abused children under age eighteen will be reduced from ten thousand to five thousand. (Linked to Results-Outcome #3)

> By the year 2000, the number of violent crimes in Division 12 will be reduced from ten thousand to five thousand. (Linked to Result-Outcome #4)

Performance measures stated without quantifiable measures to guide general policy and resource allocation decisions will be insufficient to guide the design of a change strategy. Common wisdom suggests that without knowing where we are going, any road will lead us there.

You will want to set performance measures at the program level. This will help carry the link between vision and action throughout the organization. A program performance measure is what must be achieved by programs or their participants in order to contribute to the achievement of a result or outcome. Program measures can be for individual programs and for initiatives involving more than one program. They too should be quantifiable.

In the aggregate, for example, it might be possible to say that a performance measure of a statewide workforce literacy program would be as follows.

> Within X years, nine thousand potentially displaced workers will gain skills, moving from Level I to Level II on the National Adult Literacy Survey (NALS) scale, so that increased productivity enables them to keep jobs paying $10 per hour. (Linked to a policy outcome on reducing the number of displaced workers)

> By year X, twenty-five hundred low-income children will be enabled by family literacy programs to start school fully ready, as measured by their kindergarten teachers. (Linked to a policy outcome on school readiness)

The process of identifying program performance measures can be an arduous one and will be iterative. It will begin by clarifying what actual performance relates to the achievement of the broader result or outcome. Cause and effect is not always obvious in public programs. Nevertheless, defining program performance measures will pay off, not only with better information for program managers but through more effective budget justifications. The trick will be to choose a few meaningful measures so that the process of tracking remains manageable. The acid test should always be: Does this measure help us to know whether or not we are achieving our desired result?

Performance measures are not workload measures, such as the number of probation officers employed to serve a population (an input) or the percentage of placements in group homes (an output). You will want to keep track of inputs and outputs in order to quantify the level of effort involved in achieving a result. But these should not substitute for measures of results.

Performance measures enable you to make the link between operations and achieving your vision. In choosing performance measures, your design team will need to identify the data needs of various stakeholders. The team will also have to identify what data have already been collected that can help measure performance, how new data will be acquired, and how current data burdens can be reduced. Although this may seem like a lot of work, once the system is developed the burden of information collection should be less than at present because your organization should stop collecting many measures unrelated to performance. A more detailed discussion of the data collection issues involved in creating a performance management system can be found later in this chapter.

Developing this foundation for accountability can reorient an entire organization by focusing all parts on achieving results rather than on performing tasks. These techniques can be extremely powerful in helping you move to a high-performing work organization. For this to be successful, however, you must also concentrate on how your organization is positioned to support performance. (See Exhibit 7.5.)

---

Performance measurement efforts can blow up when you least expect it. Richard Greene and Katherine Barrett unearthed these recommendations for avoiding pitfalls from the hundreds of interviews and detailed surveys they use to grade cities and states on efficient management for *Financial World* magazine (Finkle, 1995b, pp. 1–2). Possible pitfalls include

*Legislative Resistance:* Lawmakers may fear they will lose power over appropriations if the debate centers on information they do not control. Program officials must explain clearly how performance measurement can be a useful budgeting tool, enabling legislators to see which programs are delivering and to cut those that are not.

*Politics-as-Usual:* Public officials hate to expose problems to their critics. It is important to work hard to garner bipartisan support, so measurement and accountability efforts are not identified too closely with one leader or party.

*Agency Fear:* You must encourage an atmosphere that rewards improvement and does not retroactively punish failures uncovered by performance measurement.

*Results That Arrive Too Slowly:* You have to balance. Take enough time to develop good measures and systems while retaining top managers' interest.

*Lack of Leadership:* Support from the top ensures that an across-the-board effort progresses and is not shunted aside.

*A Bored or Angry Press:* Get to know individual reporters and guide them to the right information.

*Unreliable Measures:* Keep adjusting, improving, and tossing out measures throughout the process.

---

**Exhibit 7.5.  Tips for Avoiding Performance Measurement Minefields.**

# CHANGES IN POLICY, PROCESSES, AND CULTURE

Defining results deals with what your organization will accomplish. Now, it is time to consider how you will get the job done. What changes in your internal policies, work processes, and the culture of your organization would better enable you to succeed?

In traditional organizations, the policies, processes, and culture were products of the old paradigm of overly prescriptive command and control. That paradigm produced narrowly defined work processes, alienation of people from their work, limited accountability, and distrust between employees and management. Experience in the public sector has demonstrated that management and employees, including union leaders, are open to new paradigms. They need to see what benefits new ways of operating will have for them.

## Defining Policy and Program Changes

By comparing the existing operation of your organization with your intended results and performance measures, you will probably find that some of the activities of your organization have no direct bearing on achieving them. Because designing a high-performance organization involves reorienting your efforts toward achieving results, these activities are good candidates for elimination or at least close scrutiny. In other cases, you may find that the goals of some programs or activities fit with your vision but that they are not producing results. These, too, deserve special scrutiny.

This could be a very difficult process for your organization. If you have managed to engage a significant group of stakeholders, and if you have chosen a strategy that involves empowering your employees, you may be able to not only minimize the impact of these changes but have the suggested changes emerge from them.

In Chapter One, we described the whirlwind efforts to change the mission and focus of the federal Bureau of Reclamation. The significant changes made in the bureau were not only endorsed by the employees, they were recommended by them. The process of change centered on a group of employees charged by the commissioner to develop recommendations. Their report was circulated and widely reviewed by all employees who were encouraged to offer their comments. As a result, the bureau

- Converted one regional office into a service center for the entire organization

- Flattened the organization, reducing layers and shifting responsibilities to field offices

- Reduced the bureau's budget

- Changed its budgeting processes to reflect reinvention

- Doubled the training budget and changed the type of training provided

- Significantly shortened review and approval processes

- Eliminated 58 percent of the bureau's internal rules and regulations

These organizational changes, no matter what process you use to generate the plan, are about the relationships people have with their work, their customers, and their external environment. They must see the reason for the change, the need for it, and the potential benefits the change offers. Some will charge forward. Others will resist. But the more people participate in the design, the more likely they will be to make it work.

## Defining Work Process Changes

In creating a high-performance organization, you will need to question whether what you are doing now has a strong relationship to achieving the outcomes you have defined and to question the way you are going about it. That is, are you doing what is right, and are you doing it right? In some cases, you will shed some strategies or programs and add new ones. In others, you may need only to change the work processes of existing programs or parts of your organization.

In the private sector, where missions, products, sales, profits, and returns on investment are commonly known, the heart of redesign is in changing work processes. Organizational changes will flow from fundamental changes in work processes. In the public sector, we have been required to create analogs to these concepts just to get to the stage of redesigning work processes. We have had to create a new approach to performance and its measurement just to know how we are doing and to show where work processes need to be changed.

When you get to the point of considering changes in work processes, you can put the experience of the private sector to work. This experience has been incorporated in a set of principles of organizational design. These principles are linked to and build upon the characteristics of high-performing work organizations discussed in Chapter One.

## Focusing on the Productivity of the Entire Organization

For an organization to be most effective, its energy must be focused on maximizing the performance of the entire organization. It is critical that each unit not optimize what they are doing to the detriment of the whole enterprise. Consider the example of making a chair. It is impossible to improve the quality of the entire chair by merely trying to improve the quality of the legs. Although the legs may be magnificent, they may not support the weight of the chair, let alone any load on the chair.

To keep the organization focused on the production of the whole and not the optimization of the parts is difficult. To do this frequently requires that all members of the organization understand the big picture so they can make decisions based on the overall mission and goals of the organization. This tenet has led many high-performing organizations to open up their communication channels and hold frequent communication meetings that allow the entire organization to understand the business conditions confronting the organization.

This principle is linked to the characteristics of high-performing organizations of being clear on their mission, defining and focusing on results, and being competitive in terms of performance.

## Minimally Specifying Rules

In high-performance organizations, people who do the work are given the maximum amount of latitude to perform their jobs. In traditional organizations, management tries to specify nearly all aspects of jobs and methods through rigid policy and procedure manuals. They hope that through the enforcement of narrowly defined rules and policies, they will ensure greater consistency and control over the operation. In reality, this frequently has the reverse effect.

This principle means that no more than is absolutely required to get a job done is specified and that all critical factors are specified. In practice, it means that work design should be precise about what must be achieved but not how it must be achieved. That is left up to the discretion of the person or group doing the work.

For example, if a manual were to be produced in a traditional work unit, it might specify the size of the margins and the size of the type, as well as the type of machine on which the work should be printed. Someone might be designated to write the manual and someone else to type it.

If the same manual were to be done in a high-performance organization, you would specify that you want a legible manual that meets the requirements of the readers. You would leave the determination and negotiation of those requirements up to the unit that is producing the manual. They would also be given the latitude to decide how the manual is to be produced.

This discretion both increases motivation and allows for changes in the process to be made to control any problems. Under the traditional scenario, if the machine broke or the typeface was not available, those in charge of the project would have no way to quickly modify the design or correct the variance.

This principle is linked to the characteristics of high-performance organizations of empowering employees and instituting new work processes to inspire and motivate people to succeed.

## Solving Problems Where They Happen

Quality control departments are passé. No longer can we rely on someone else to check for our mistakes. We each need to be accountable for the quality of our functions. Quality departments and "inspector general" offices arose in part because, in an effort to mass produce and bureaucratically control, we alienated people from their work and destroyed a natural sense of accountability. Work redesign is an attempt to put that feedback and accountability back into the work so that problems can be controlled where they happen.

This principle recognizes each individual as the front line of defense for his or her task and the manager as the front line of defense for boundary-spanning tasks or tasks that involve management between functions. This principle says that responsibility needs to lie with the person who does the work. For example, by integrating quality-control functions into work teams at Northern Telecom's Morrisville plant, the number of full-time quality inspectors dropped by 40 percent, and the number of quality problems dropped by 50 percent.

This principle, as is the one before it, is linked to the characteristics of high-performance organizations of empowering employees and instituting new work processes to inspire and motivate people to succeed.

Develop employees who are multiskilled, knowledgeable about the business, and highly flexible. There are tremendous advantages in having employees who are multiskilled and capable of performing a variety of jobs and functions. By having a multiskilled workforce, disruptions due to absenteeism, changes in demand, and equipment failure can be more effectively and expediently addressed. It is also more motivating to perform a job that has multiple tasks (what is referred to in the job design literature as "skill variety"). And when employees understand the business of the enterprise, it is easier for them to make decisions that are in line with its strategic direction.

In one hotel chain, the usual job categories of housekeeper, room service provider, and bell person were all combined, and a multiskilled team in which each member was capable of performing all the tasks was created and called the "guest services team." To accomplish this, they needed to work closely with the union to redefine job specifications and to work with the resistance that was created around tipping. Some of the original jobs were high-tip jobs, while others received no tips. With the new constellation, the tips were shared by more people.

This principle is linked to the characteristics of high-performing work organizations of empowering employees and being flexible, adaptable, and quick to adjust when conditions change.

### Directing Information Flow to the Point Where Direct Action Can Be Taken

In a traditional organization, information often goes up the hierarchical ladder where a decision maker makes a decision. Then it goes back down the ladder to a worker who acts on the decision. For example, if you were running a food service operation, a cook may keep track of how much hamburger was used and then submit a report to a manager. The manager would then gather information about the price of meat from various wholesalers, record this month's hamburger orders, compare them to last month's orders, and then make a decision about the order. In a high-performance organization, the cook would have access to the trend data, understand what changes may be affecting it, and order the meat directly.

The information flow should provide people at all levels with adequate information to make daily decisions on how to improve the performance of their work and solve problems that directly affect them.

This principle also is linked to the characteristics of high-performance organizations of empowering employees and being flexible, adaptable, and quick to adjust when conditions change.

## Building Support Systems That Support the Work Design

The management systems should be designed to reinforce the behaviors intended by the new structure. Rewards, hiring practices, departmental structure, training systems, and so on all need to be congruent with the basic work design and work group structure. For example, it would be incongruent to reward narrow skill specialization if one were striving for multiskilled workers.

This principle is linked to the characteristic of high-performance organizations of empowering employees and restructuring work processes to meet customer needs.

## Adopting a High Quality of Work Life as a Core Value

Organizations are most effective when they achieve their objectives while meeting the needs of their employees. A principle of work redesign is that superior results come from the joint optimization of individual and organizational needs. The workplace of the future can no longer be only a place to receive a paycheck. The workplace must foster personal development, growth, and education. It is the only way that we will be able to stay competitive.

This principle is linked to the characteristic of high-performance organizations of empowering employees and maintaining open, productive communications.

In addition to these work process changes, you will also want to consider the culture of your organization. You have already assessed the culture of your organization. Now you should consider any changes you want to make in your organization's culture to help boost performance.

## Changing the Culture

The culture of an organization is the sum total of its ways of operating and working together. The culture of an organization is reflected in its values. Changing the culture of the organization is critical for a shift to high performance. Remember that high-performance organizations change the relationship between people and their work, organizations and their customers, and organizations and their internal environment. These changes involve significant shifts in ways of operating and working together.

One way of changing the culture is by focusing the organization on performance as it relates to a vision and benchmarks. Another is to clarify your values and to review operating processes and procedures in terms of them. Still another is to change the way work is organized. Each of the strategies discussed earlier in this chapter will have significant implications for your organization's culture. If, for example, you choose the route of total quality management, your culture will shift to a cooperative approach, including quality circles as methods of operation. If you choose a strategy of empowering your customers, the way your organization operates and works together will shift to be more responsive to your customers.

One of the most important issues to consider in changing the culture of your organization is diversity. There is widespread agreement that the workforce composition is changing. The Department of Labor and Hudson Institute's Work Force 2000 report forecast dramatic workforce shifts by the year 2000. According to the report, nearly 85 percent of the 25 million workers entering the labor pool will be women, minorities, or immigrants. The total share of the workforce made up of white men would decline from 51 percent to 45 percent. Subsequent studies by the U.S. Department of Labor have confirmed these trend lines.

Although these facts are agreed upon, there is disagreement about their implications. Some companies maintain that there is no need to alter internal operating policies and procedures simply because workforce demographics are changing. Other companies disagree, and disagree strongly.

Companies that have made managing diversity a priority—companies like Xerox, AT&T, IBM, and Levi Strauss—say they have done so for several reasons:

*Recruiting.* Companies listed as "best places to work" for women and minorities are able to attract the top talent in this large and growing pool of employees.

*Retention.* The companies also assert that systems designed when employees were almost exclusively white and male will not fit the needs or tastes of a more diverse group. Similarly, they are concerned about extensive data showing that existing systems favor promotion of white males, particularly into executive ranks. (Despite increased representation of women and minorities in management for several decades, 96 percent of senior executive positions are held by white males.) This so-called glass ceiling effect causes women and minorities to leave the organization in disproportionate numbers. Numerous studies show that lack of promotional opportunities is a major cause of exit for women and minorities in our existing organizations.

*Marketing.* As an IBM executive puts it, "We think it is important for our customers to look inside and see people like them. If they cannot, it seems to me that the prospect of them becoming or staying our customer declines."

*Representation.* For public sector organizations, it may be particularly important to reflect the demographics of constituents at all levels of the hierarchy. Citizens may be unlikely to believe government has their interests at heart if it has few or no members of various ethnic or cultural groups within its employee ranks or if they are found at only the lowest levels of the hierarchy.

*Performance.* There is some evidence that diverse teams outperform homogeneous teams. In a recent study at the University of North Texas, ethnically diverse teams of business students were pitted without their knowledge against all-white teams for seventeen weeks. At first, homogeneous teams sprinted ahead. But by the study's end, the heterogeneous groups were viewing situations from a broader range of perspectives and producing more innovative solutions to problems. Researchers on business process reengineering and other high-performance efforts find the most successful efforts to recast an organization's performance come when individuals from different units work together to define and recast current practices. Similarly, research on the Myers-Briggs personality test indicates that when a task is novel or when the environment is rapidly changing, heterogeneous groups outperform homogeneous groups. Although this evidence is not conclusive, it does suggest that there may be previously unrecognized benefits to a diverse workforce.

The fact remains, however, that our workplace is becoming more diverse. High-performance organizations will build their cultures to take advantage of the benefits of diversity.

# SELECTING STRATEGIES FOR CHANGE

Alternative strategies have been used in the public sector to help organizations boost their performance. The major strategies are discussed next. These strategies are not mutually exclusive; each has its strengths and weaknesses. Each is more or less attractive to the people in an organization, depending on their culture and history and the external climate for change. You may want to combine approaches or elements of many. But always remember to keep the primary focus on the vision of the organization and measure the utility of the approach against what you are trying to achieve.

## Total Quality Management

Creech (1994) describes the management philosophy espoused by W. Edwards Deming as involving an orientation to quality throughout the organization or business. It takes a humanistic approach to the way employees are treated, seeking to empower workers at all levels, particularly the front line. It is also holistic, applying its principles organizationwide. Because of its widespread adoption in the private sector, TQM now encompasses a broad array of quality-oriented management practices. The TQM approach involves clearly defining goals and tasks but moving away from large, centrally managed operations to smaller, team-based organizing units (see also George, 1994).

## Business Process Reengineering

"Reengineering is the fundamental rethinking and radical redesign of business processes to achieve dramatic improvements in critical, contemporary measures of performance—measures such as cost, quality, service, and speed" (Hammer and Champy, 1993, p. 32). Reengineering organizations involves a complete makeover based on the question: If I were creating this company today, given what I know and given current technology, what would it look like? (Hammer and Champy, 1993, p. 31). Business process engineering requires that current organizational structure, resources, and work processes be set aside and that the designer simply start over, designing the new organization based on most current knowledge, skills, and technologies (see also Caudle, 1994).

## Principle-Driven Change

Some strategies for change involve focusing on an agreed-upon set of principles to guide a change process—principles such as decentralization, deregulation, customer focus, employee incentives, or doing more with the same or fewer resources. This strategy involves attempting to change operating policies and procedures to make them coherent with these principles. This was the strategy used in the first round of the National Performance Review (NPR). The second round of the NPR process added another dimension to this approach. It questioned the value of performing certain functions, even if they had been made consistent with these principles. This evolution illustrates that whatever strategy you choose for change, you must keep in mind your vision or reason for change. Otherwise, you could end up operating more efficiently but performing irrelevant functions.

## Privatization

Based on the assumption that the private sector can provide public services more efficiently and at less cost than government, some elected and appointed officials have embraced a strategy of privatization. Privatization involves transferring responsibility for the delivery of certain government services to the private sector under contract with government. This has occurred in many government services, ranging from trash removal to the operation of correctional facilities. This strategy is consistent with the values of limiting the size of government and taking advantage of market forces to provide more cost-effective services.

## Competition

Some of those involved in the process of moving toward high performance feel strongly that the real challenge is to make government more competitive, with both the private sector and with itself. Osborne and Gaebler (1992) suggest that monopoly has become the American way in government. Competition among service providers offers a strategy for keeping costs down and meeting customer needs in a timely way. "Competition in government . . . drives us to embrace innovation and strive for excellence" (Osborne and Gaebler, 1992, p. 79).

These are strategies for helping you fulfill your vision and mission. Your choice of which to employ should be a function of how they fit with your values in order to help you fulfill your vision and measurable goals. They are not the same as the steps of change to be discussed next that you will go through to implement your vision. You should keep these strategies in mind, however, as you begin to quantify your vision. You may not want to commit yourself to a particular strategy until after you have defined your outcomes. However, there may be stated or unstated strategies such as privatization or competition that have permeated the change process from the beginning. If this is the case, you should openly recognize these operating strategies for achieving change and reconsider the emphasis you want to place on them.

## IMPLEMENTING, COMMUNICATING, EVALUATING, AND CONTINUOUSLY IMPROVING

By now you should be relatively well versed on the nature of high-performance organizations and how you go about creating them. You should be almost ready to embark on your own change effort. Before doing so, however, you will want to familiarize yourself with those tasks related to implementation, communication, evaluation, and continuous improvement.

### Implementation: Building a Performance Management System

An important aspect of implementing a high-performance workplace is putting in place a performance management system that will enable you to measure performance, report results, and improve performance continuously. Such a system also tells you some critical things about the resources devoted to these efforts and how they are organized. With this information, you will be better able to tell which types of programs are best suited to assist your citizens.

These steps flow naturally from the development of performance measures discussed earlier in this chapter. Key steps in building a performance management system follow.

*Negotiate data collection protocols with service providers and other data sources.* Your plan for change should attend to the process through which the design team intends to develop a cooperative data collection system. You should develop sample reports for different stakeholders and lists of those data items to be added, those to be continued, and those to be dropped (see Exhibit 7.6). From these products, the design team can get a good idea of how difficult it will be to engage the organization and its service providers in providing reliable data on a regular basis. A note of caution: where data collection is not readily agreed to, the data will be suspect or possibly useless. The landscape is littered with ill-advised attempts to get field personnel, who are legitimately more worried about service provision than reporting, to provide accurate data. If they do not see the relevance of the reporting to their own lives, data collection may break down.

*Collect data.* Data collection will begin after the plan for change has been adopted. The design team will want to work with each agency and a pilot or group of pilot agencies in the field to work out the bugs

---

The logic of conducting results measurement is compelling, but your measurement systems may not be ready for the task. A reliable performance management system requires several types of data:

*Small area data* tell us about people in their communities. Census track data are too broad.

*Frequently gathered data* are necessary so that changes in increments of one year or less can be monitored. Five- and ten-year increments are not sufficient.

*Longitudinal data* allow the tracking of progress over time to determine the long-term effect of a strategy or program.

*Customer satisfaction data* help gauge the public's perception of progress, their confidence in government services, and their overall sense of well-being.

*Effective practice data,* based more on evaluation research and less on anecdote, help us understand the strengths and weaknesses of various strategies.

*Common client data* help clarify the progress of people who are receiving multiple services delivered through multiple systems.

---

**Exhibit 7.6.    A Note on the Limits of Data.**

in the data collection system negotiated in the previous step. Over time, the performance management system will generate actual data with which to fill in the sample reports. As this process occurs, the design team can check once again with the audiences, fine-tuning the output.

*Test the system.* Using "mocked-up" data, you should test the data system by showing reports and other communications vehicles to customers before they have actual, useful data to report. This will enable customers of the system—audience by audience—to refine the method and type of communication before the actual data are available.

*Report results.* As the system is phased in, results will begin to be available for reporting to each audience. During the strategic planning process, the team will want to consider carefully not only how the reports will be generated but how they will be communicated to broader audiences such as the public and the press. In addition, the team will want to find ways to use the information generated to feed back information in training and professional development contexts to the field. Because an essential purpose of a performance management system is to provide information that will lead to a process of quality improvement, this function will be crucial in the long run.

The performance management system should show clearly where resources are insufficient to achieve program and policy outcomes. Similarly, it should be possible to identify certain crucial processes in programs that must be present for program outcomes to be achieved. These can then inform the standard-setting processes already at work at the federal, state, and local levels. The system should also help you identify those resources, program elements, population characteristics, and other factors that can be shown to hold back a particular program from meeting its goals or help it to succeed. Identifying these constraints and enablers is finding out what works under what conditions and then applying that knowledge.

In the public sector, the difficulty of developing a performance management system and, in particular, rationalizing the data collection and reporting systems must not be underestimated (see Exhibit 7.7). At the state level, experience in states such as Texas and Oregon underscore that this is a multiyear process. Data elements currently collected by government have grown up over the years in response to many different laws and regulations. They overlap. They leave large gaps in information. They are inconsistent with each other. The time frames for their collection differ. Laws govern what can be shared and under what

The National Institute for Literacy initiated a five-state process to develop performance management systems. States included in this process were Tennessee, Kentucky, Hawaii, New York, and Alabama. Early experience garnered from these states and from the states of Texas and Oregon is summarized below (Campbell and Foster, 1995).

- There must be strong direction and commitment from the top.
- Staff and resource commitments are large, and they change in nature over time.
- Use externally imposed deadlines to move the process along.
- Involve the potential audiences for information early in the process.
- Do not expect perfect outcome measures the first time. Focus on a process of continuous improvement.
- Link performance measures directly to vision, benchmarks, and outcomes.
- Balance the use of existing performance measures and developing new, more precise measures.
- Consider the full implications of standardizing data collection and reporting across agencies and programs.

**Exhibit 7.7.   Developing Performance Management Systems.**

circumstances. These are formidable, but not insurmountable, obstacles to developing performance measures that track progress to achieving results. You should just understand that sorting through this maze and rationalizing it will probably take several years. Putting this system in place will enable you to fully implement your move toward high performance.

## Developing a Communications Strategy

As you proceed with your move to a high-performance organization, you will need to develop a communications strategy that will enable you to communicate the results of your efforts with stakeholders and to continue to build support. A communications strategy is a critical part of the change process.

The process of effective change to a high-performing work organization is people-centered. It is about changing the attitudes and behaviors of those within the organization and even its other stakeholders. To help them with this transition, you must be able to keep them apprised of the changes that are occurring, keep them involved in the process of change, and help them become contributing members of your organization's process of continuous improvement.

DEFINE YOUR AUDIENCES. The key to designing a useful communications strategy is to define your audiences carefully and to customize your communications vehicles so that you can give each audience concise information in an easily accessible format. Customized communications vehicles might be appropriate for the following types of audiences:

• *Governmental officials.* The governor, mayor, legislative leaders, city council, county executive, cabinet officials, and the directors of affected agencies should receive regular communications of results. In addition, they should be briefed about what the changes mean and how this information can be used to adjust policy to better accomplish the organization's mission.

• *Other agency managers.* Managers of programs or agencies also need to receive information on what works and what does not. But the level of detail and the focus will differ from that targeted to the elected and appointed officials.

• *Other employees.* In a high-performance organization where employees are empowered to make more decisions on their own, they will need up-to-date information on which to base their decisions. If the mission, values, and goals of your organization are to be kept uppermost in the minds of employees, a communications strategy must be in place to ensure that these foundation pieces are not lost in a day-to-day scramble of operations.

• *Providers, including direct service providers.* Providers need to know how they are doing and how their peers are doing in improving their performance under the new system.

• *Unions.* Unions can be valuable supporters of a change process if they are involved in the change process and assured that the benefits of the change are shared in some way with their members. Your communications system must keep union leaders and members abreast of changes, the impact of these changes on them, and progress in achieving goals.

• *Interest groups.* In the process of moving to a high-performance organization, you will probably identify a substantial number of citizens' groups and organizations not directly engaged in making policy or in providing services but who are concerned about your organization. A communications system should provide the information they need to see progress, identify problems, and know where they can be of help.

• *Customers.* Your customers deserve to know what changes are taking place in your agency. They may not want to be burdened with much detail, but they should be made aware of progress the organization is making and how it will affect them or improve service.

**TAILOR YOUR COMMUNICATIONS VEHICLES TO YOUR AUDIENCES.** In communicating the nature and results of your efforts with the types of people just listed, it will be important to tailor these communications to the precise needs of each. Several types of vehicles could be considered.

• *Prepare standard report templates for elected and appointed officials.* The governor, mayor, city council, legislators, and other state and local officials can be reached with simple and colorful graphics showing the results of your organization's efforts. These need not be fancy but must be arresting, and they must show progress and resources devoted to addressing priority issues. This report can be designed in concert with the budget or planning office.

• *Organize a task force of program managers to design their own report.* Involving the users in the design of program manager reports will ensure that they get what they need to improve program performance. This communications vehicle may be more complex than others, but it should still be focused directly on the mission and achieving the goals.

• *Organize providers to assist in designing communications vehicles and ways to share innovations.* Service providers could be polled concerning the types of information they would like to have in a simple one- or two-page report. A newsletter format might be useful so that innovations could be shared in addition to data from the performance management system.

• *Prepare a video explaining important changes and results.* A video could provide a general introduction to the high-performance organization and an overview of the benefits to the stakeholders. It could be used for presentations to legislative and civic leaders.

• *Design a community report.* The results of the high-performance organization can be summarized and reported to the community in a variety of ways; it can be done electronically, or in brochures, or through other media.

• *Provide periodic feedback to employees.* Many different types of communications vehicles can be used to communicate the results of your shift to high performance to employees. These can include union newsletters, briefings, group discussions, staff meetings, and periodic employee conferences.

## Evaluating and Continuously Improving

The data emerging from your performance management system should reveal gaps in program coverage and areas where additional investments should be made to improve performance. Although resources may not be available immediately, plans for continuous improvement can be developed that will enable program managers and others to invest any additional resources effectively. Data from this system will not automatically lead to these investments, but they will provide a firmer foundation for justifying new investments. You may want to review the discussion on investment decision making in Chapter Nine to understand the link between information emerging from a performance management system and an investment-oriented budgeting system. Information from a performance management system also should allow program providers to reallocate personnel and other resources at the program level to improve efficiency and effectiveness.

In building a sound base of accountability through the strategic planning process, we will have information that

Enables us to see whether we are achieving our goals

Helps us advocate more effectively for resources

Gives us good information about the best places to invest those resources

Enables service providers to receive much more flexible funding in return for achieving measurable results

Helps us explain to the legislature, press, and public where we are making progress in meeting our goals and where we need to do more work

The ultimate purpose of these steps in the move toward high performance is to provide us with the information we need to engage in a process of continuous improvement. By focusing on results rather than process alone, we will be able to adjust our resources—financial and human—to make the most progress possible toward our vision.

Most of the examples of shifts to high performance found in the public sector focus on the role of the executive branch. The legislative branch can be a very powerful force for change as well. Discussions with legislators and city council members have resulted in some advice about the roles that legislators might play.

In moving toward high performance, for example, the legislative branch could represent the voice of the customer in the planning process, facilitate an information exchange between the public and the government, and serve an integrating function within the public sector and to other sectors. In terms of their decision-making responsibilities, a strategic vision can be an excellent tool for helping to make difficult choices and could help legislators move away from across-the-board budget cuts and other untargeted decisions.

A high-performance work environment could help the legislative branch become more investment-oriented and more inclined to work as a catalyst for change. A focus on high performance could enable legislative branch members to better allocate their time away from fighting "brush fires" toward a focus on systems. Finally, in a high-performance environment, members of the legislative branch might consider spending more time focusing on how to support intrapreneurship and developing new approaches to rewarding and keeping employees with these skills.

If our organizations are to become more high performing, we will eventually have to move beyond the level of one program or agency to a more systemwide approach. We must learn to view programs as a means to an end. Some programs stand alone. Others may need to operate as pieces of a strategy. Several programs operating in several agencies might work in tandem in order to achieve results such as decreasing teen pregnancy or enhancing adult literacy.

As a step toward aligning agencies, programs, and resources with your intended results, you might address these questions:

1. What will it take to influence results? What combination of actions would likely make a difference?

2. Which existing programs, on their own or in combination, have potential to influence the results we hope to achieve?

3. What would enable us to deploy these programs more effectively as common elements of a larger strategy to achieve our results? Common eligibility requirements? Reporting requirements? Definitions? Planning cycles? Blended funds? Can these be achieved? Through what means?

4. Who is responsible for implementing these programs, and what authority do they have to operate more flexibly?

The answers to these questions are important to building a strategy for results. They allow you to chart programs and resources, assess their strengths, and identify gaps.

Although this kind of alignment is logical, it is difficult to accomplish. One reason is that the incompatibility of agencies and programs is often a function of statutory, not administrative, limitations. Another reason has to do with the strong influence of central management systems in government. The next four chapters will help you think through the issues involved in revamping primary central management systems—budget, human resources, and procurement—to foment and support high performance.

## ACCOUNTABILITY AND CONSEQUENCES

What happens if the effort is successful? If the partners achieve results on time and under budget, what are the rewards? Conversely, what happens if they do not? What if little progress is made and the costs are high? What are the penalties? And in a partnership model, who determines rewards and penalties? (See Exhibit 7.8.)

## ESTABLISHING REWARDS AND PENALTIES

We have not traditionally dealt well with rewards and penalties in government. Although some programs grant authority to issue sanctions to grantees who do not comply with standards, these have rarely been issued. We do have a tradition of perverse consequences for operating

---

1. What do you want to benchmark?

2. How is your organization doing? What does your process look like? What do you want your system to do? How is your department structured?

3. Which organization does best at that particular activity? (For example, L. L. Bean might be best at warehousing and distribution.)

4. Is this organization really better? If so, how much better?
   Why are they better? What can we learn from them?
   How can we apply what we learned to our agency?

5. How will we integrate what we have learned into our planning? How will we integrate these findings into our organization's goals?

6. What are the keys to implementing, measuring, and refining the ideas we learned?

---

**Exhibit 7.8.    Six Questions to Guide Benchmarking Efforts.**

*Source:* Resnick-West, 1994, p. 12.

efficiently. If we spend less to achieve a task, we get our budget cut next time around.

In this period of transition, policymakers are attempting to develop more effective rewards and penalties. For example, in Oregon's welfare waiver, the state can keep some of the funds saved from reducing case loads to reinvest in its program. This is a revenue-neutral financial reward for success. Other types of financial incentives, recognition, increasing flexibility, and professional advancement are among the rewards that could be considered.

There are two types of failure. One is when partners fail to live up to their commitments, use poor judgment, or act dishonestly. For these there should be clear and immediate consequences such as making leadership and personnel changes, redirecting or reducing funds, imposing more stringent requirements, or even terminating the partnership.

The other is failure to achieve a result due to setting overly ambitious goals, unforeseen changes in circumstances, or other conditions outside the partners' span of influence. For this type of failure there should be opportunities to learn, make course corrections, and improve.

Still to be resolved is the question of how intergovernmental partners share risk and rewards as equals. Because we have no precedent for rewards and penalties in a results-driven partnership, those involved in these early experiments must begin to develop the protocols.

---

*Benchmark (private sector):* Performance comparisons of organizational business processes against an internal or external standard of recognized leaders. Most often the comparison is made against a similar process in another organization considered world class.

*Benchmark (public sector):* A measurable statement of a condition that must exist to achieve a vision, that is, a statement of where we want to be in the future. Benchmarks provide measurable markers along the way toward achieving the specifics of the vision. A benchmark is usually stated in terms of a rate. This use of the term *benchmarks* should not be confused with the common use of the term in the corporate world, where benchmarks are industry standards of excellence.

*Business Process:* A collection of related, structured activities—a chain of events—that produces a specific service or product for a particular customer or customers.

*Business Process Reengineering:* In government, a radical improvement approach that critically examines, rethinks, and redesigns mission-delivery processes and subprocesses, achieving dramatic mission performance gains from multiple customer and stakeholder perspectives.

---

**Exhibit 7.9.   Glossary of Terms
for Developing a Plan for Change.**

*Constraints and Enablers:* Factors that can help or hinder a program or policy in achieving the desired outcomes.

*Culture:* All the things that a group of people inhabiting an organization do, the ways they do things, and the ways they think and feel about them.

*Customer:* Groups or individuals who have a business relationship with the organization, including direct recipients of products and services, internal customers who produce services and products for final recipients, and other organizations and entities that interact with an organization to produce products and services.

*Feedback and Continuous Improvement:* A process through which policymakers, program managers, service providers, and other stakeholders learn from associating indicators of program quality with data on outcomes achieved. Improvement occurs when this information is used to adjust programs to increase their productivity and the quality of outcomes.

*Inputs:* Resources devoted to program interventions or policies. They may include staff, facilities, utilities, material, and other resources. Training, for example, is an input.

*Outcome:* A quantifiable change in conditions or circumstances that result from one or a combination of interventions.

*Outputs:* The volume of activity generated by a program or strategy. The numbers of people completing a training program is an example of an output.

*Performance Measures:* Quantifiable measures of whether policies or programs are contributing to the achievement of policy or program outcomes. These can be expressed either in absolute numbers or in terms of rates and should be available at regular intervals. A performance measure shows progress (or lack of it) in achieving the outcome. Performance measures may be proxies for achievement of policy or program outcomes.

*Process:* The interaction between the people served by a program and the inputs or resources devoted to that program.

*Program Intervention:* An action or actions by government, for-profit or nonprofit organization, or other provider of services designed to achieve a program outcome. This usually is a service program but can also include various regulatory, job-related, or tax incentives for individual action.

*Program Outcomes:* The results of program interventions aimed at achieving policy outcomes, usually stated in terms of the numbers of individual outcomes achieved by a specific time in the near future.

*Stakeholder Analysis:* The identification of individuals or groups that can affect or be affected by a given issue. An understanding of various constituency attitudes and beliefs regarding the issues of concern and how they may be helped or harmed by actions taken in relation to the issue.

*Stakeholders:* People or organizations whose lives will be affected by policies, programs, or the achievement of benchmarks or whose decisions will affect policies, programs, or the achievement of benchmarks.

**Exhibit 7.9.    Glossary of Terms
for Developing a Plan for Change (*continued*).**

*Standards of Program Quality:* A list of specific elements of programs that are thought to be crucial for the programs' success and without which the likelihood of program success is small. These can be inputs or processes that are known to be associated with positive outcomes.

*Target Population:* A group of people with similar characteristics who are deemed a high priority to benefit from policies and programs. Identifying target populations is usually required to achieve a program or policy outcome and, ultimately, to achieve benchmarks.

*Total Quality Management:* A systemic effort to analyze the performance of an organization with the goal of improving quality. This management philosophy was espoused by W. Edwards Deming and involves an orientation to quality throughout the organization or business. It is a humanistic approach to the way employees are treated and to the empowerment of workers at all levels, particularly the front line; it is a holistic application that is organizationwide.

*Vision:* A compelling, inspiring picture of a possible and preferred future.

*Vision Statement:* A vision statement is a concise statement of the conditions and the quality of life that citizens in a state or community want to see in the future.

**Exhibit 7.9.    Glossary of Terms
for Developing a Plan for Change *(continued)*.**

# PART THREE

# Strengthening Central Management Systems to Support High Performance

# CHAPTER EIGHT

# An Introduction to High-Performance Central Management Systems

N<sub></sub> o one would expect the U.S. Army to fight with the same weapons, tactics, training, delegations of authority, and rules of engagement today as it did in the Civil War. . . . In many parts of domestic government, however, we are still using tactics, weaponry, delegation of authority, and rules of engagement that we used more than fifty years ago" (Leonard, Cook, and McNeil, 1995, p. 14).

As you work toward high performance in your public agency, some of the thorniest challenges you will confront are presented by overly prescriptive rules imposed by unyielding central management systems. Innovators from across the country and from all levels of government can share myriad stories of how their reform efforts were stymied by bureaucracy and inflexible management systems.

Central management systems pose different obstacles, depending on where you find yourself in the government system. From the perspective of the consumers of government services, central management agencies responsible for administrative activities such as budgeting and personnel are seemingly irrelevant—until you consider the toll they take when they hinder innovation and dampen agency performance.

From the perspective of a provider of service, these central management activities are sources of occasional irritation, particularly during procurement processes.

Central management agencies—whether they are federal, state, or local—are likely to be blamed for delaying action and increasing costs. If you are a program manager or an elected or appointed policymaker, central management agencies and the requirements they impose are both convenient scapegoats and real obstacles to change.

From the perspectives of the governor, the federal cabinet official, and the state or federal legislative leaders, however, central management agencies provide the lifeblood of governance—centralized information and control. As a result, these agencies and the central management activities they perform are very powerful and are often wedded to the status quo.

Leaders in both the legislative and executive branches appreciate the ability of central management agencies to slow down spending, make it difficult to hire a new employee, or require paperwork from line agencies. None of these acts are appreciated alone. But they do help control spending and provide centralized information needed to manage and make policy decisions. In most cases, political leaders are willing to put up with the negatives to get the positives.

Recognizing this important relationship between political leaders and their central management agencies, how can we change those agencies so that they are less burdensome to program managers and service providers, and, at the same time, improve the accountability in the system? How can we help reform central budgeting, personnel, or procurement processes, for example, so that they serve not only those above them but also their peers in agencies and those on the front lines of service delivery? This is the challenge of reforming our central management systems while reaching for high performance in the public sector.

Your organization or agency, whether it is a small bureau or a mega-department, may survive these mounting challenges of the day. It may even weather new pressures that are likely to emerge in the decades ahead. They are, however, less likely to thrive or reach the highest possible level of performance in achieving their missions.

Bob Stone, project director of the National Performance Review, shares insights on the goals and focus of their reinvention effort:

At the beginning of NPR, there was a lot of talk about the supposed tension between the goals of making government work better and making it cost less. Some people thought the goal to cut 250,000 federal employees was driven by politicians. In fact, much of the passion for reducing the federal workforce came from civil servants who chafed under central management control and micromanagement in government. When we counted up federal civil employees, we found that 660,000 of the 2,000,000 were overseeing, second guessing, and managing the people who do the work. The basic rule of reform is to do something about the people who are keeping people from getting their jobs done. The challenge is to get the blocking forces out of the way [Stone, 1995].

The core administrative and management systems of our public sector organizations such as budget, personnel, and procurement systems reflect their origins. They were set (and reformed and set again) to manage the burgeoning bureaucracies of the late nineteenth and early twentieth centuries.

These systems are based on and emphasize control by central authorities, strict and confining limits on the production or delivery process, and atomization of tasks. The people at the top are the primary, if not the sole, decision makers. Multiple layers of middle managers hold authority over operations, albeit within prescribed limits. And too many front line-workers confront a numbingly invariable range of tasks and standardized routines in their daily work. Their focus is circumscribed, and they are given little responsibility for determining the best way to get their jobs done. Their ideas are seldom sought and, even less frequently, acted upon.

How can we improve the performance of the public sector? One inviting source of ideas and techniques for doing so is the experience of American businesses. Much can be learned by public leaders from the transformation efforts under way in the private sector. During the 1980s, many American enterprises discovered that mass production systems created during the era of rapid industrialization are ill suited to today's production challenges and market opportunities.

There is ample evidence as well that the business methods of many of our public sector organizations may be incapable of supporting the level of effective, long-term performance that the public is demanding and that committed professionals at all levels seek to achieve.

Our challenge is to develop and implement reforms that can help transform organizational cultures and the budget, human resource, and procurement systems we have put in place. Many American businesses are creating new systems to respond to increasing competitive pressures and changing markets. They are reinventing management structures, pruning prescriptive rules, flattening hierarchies, and empowering the men and women on the front line. And they are redesigning processes from the production on the shop floor to research at the laboratory bench.

Most important, we must develop strategies that help central management systems make the transition from excessive micromanagement. We must reform them in such a way that they make the maximum possible contribution to the agency's core mission. This entails a shift from viewing these systems as control structures and organizational overhead to vital contributors that add value toward achievement of our organizational missions.

The public sector can and is learning from the experience of their private sector counterparts. Change is also being pushed by leaders, including agency heads, case workers, politicians, and career civil servants, from within our government agencies. Change is all around us. It has become our expectation for government as well.

In the next three chapters, we invite you to explore what three different high-performing central management systems might look like, that is, their characteristics and criteria for developing their *budgeting systems, human resource management systems,* and *procurement systems.*

# CHAPTER NINE

# High-Performance Budgeting Systems

udgeting systems for all our public organizations face the same challenges. Whether the system serves a multi-billion-dollar state government, serves a public welfare agency committing hundreds of millions of taxpayer dollars, or governs the tens of thousands spent to ensure that our city's refuse is properly disposed, the challenge is the same.

With limited funds and a virtually insatiable demand for services, public resources must be allocated to meet the public's priorities. Spending rules must be set and enforced, and oversight must ensure that public funds are not misspent. Yet, current fiscal systems present some roadblocks to improved governmental performance.

Increasingly in the 1990s, our public budgeting systems are called upon to achieve much more. Ensuring that public funds are not misspent is woefully inadequate. The public outcry and our commitment to meeting pressing social and economic problems make it essential that taxpayer funds must be spent well.

Osborne and Gaebler (1992, p. 161) conclude that "in government, the most important lever—the system that drives behavior most powerfully—is the budget." Budgeting is almost always the single most important policy action taken each year. In very powerful ways, the budget process both reflects and shapes the culture and incentives within our organizations. Revamping budget systems is an integral step toward improving effectiveness and sustaining high performance.

## CRITERIA FOR HIGH-PERFORMANCE BUDGET SYSTEMS

George Delaney, Colorado's state planning and budget director, provides an important perspective on budgeting systems in the public sector. He suggests: "There are many rational budgeting systems. . . . However, the political environment is dynamic and fluid, and often results in decisions which are neither completely rational or systematic. This does not mean that such systems should not be employed. Only that we should not become so enchanted with the rational systems that we fail to recognize the constraints the governmental budget environment has on a 'chosen' system" (Delaney, 1995).

Changes in central management systems can both enable innovation and challenge innovators to be ever more creative, responsive, and responsible. The task of reform is not small. But neither is the potential payoff from the effort. Our challenge is to make practical choices and to chart a course that can move us from where we are to where we want to be.

To begin reforming existing budgeting systems, you must start with a clear understanding of both the traditional and the new performance goals that should be set. Our traditional budgeting systems were formulated to meet a demanding set of objectives. A list of these objectives, as adapted from Miller (1992, p. 228), includes *financial control, comprehensiveness, accuracy-clarity, rationality, dependability,* and *annuality.*

What is needed today includes these characteristics, along with a new set of objectives suited to supporting high performance. The budget cycle and the budgetary process must be capable of coping with the governmental problems at hand. This means there must be an emphasis on flexibility and adaptability, not an emphasis on an idea that is intended to be unchanging.

## CHARACTERISTICS OF A NEW PARADIGM BUDGET SYSTEM

What characteristics are needed in a budgeting system for a high-performance public organization? The key characteristics or principles that leading theorists and practitioners identify are *accountability, consequences, flexibility, longer time frame,* and *strategic insights.*

## Accountability

Accountability is a keystone of a budget system supporting the transformation to a high-performance organization. The challenge is to move beyond the traditional "bean counting" mentality.

New systems in high-performance organizations should allow authority over some fiscal decisions to be moved to the most appropriate levels. And in the bargain, we must hold those officials responsible for producing real results that matter rather than slavish adherence to procedures and processes that have only the most tenuous linkage to outcomes.

As Miller (1992, p. 229) proposes, "The proper stewardship of public funds must emphasize the rigorous evaluation of the efficiency and effectiveness of operations and of the highest quality end products possible."

Making the shift will require policymakers to make tough decisions in setting priorities and defining very clearly the desired outcomes. We also need to develop incentives in the system to ensure that all levels focus on results—from the top of the agency to the front line, from the legislative appropriations committees to the nonprofit organizations that provide direct services (see Exhibit 9.1).

---

1. Who is accountable? Is accountability fixed with one agency or bureau? Or is it spread across systems or across governments?

2. For what outcomes or results are they accountable? What are the outcomes and performance indicators? Are the data reliable? Are data available at the right level? Can data be reported frequently—monthly or quarterly?

3. What sources of funding will be used? Is a single source of funding involved or are packages of funding sources possible to create incentives for better performance?

4. What standards or safeguards will be used? Have you reached agreement on the definition of performance and how it is to be measured and reported? Have you set reasonable boundaries for responsibility?

5. What are the risks, rewards, and penalties? Are risks and rewards reasonably balanced?

6. What period of time is covered? Does the agreement allow enough time for demonstrating the achievement of desired results?

---

**Exhibit 9.1.   Six Key Questions for Creating a New Deal:
Trading Accountability for Fund Flexibility.**

*Source:* Adapted from Friedman, 1996, p. 15.

Osborne emphasizes the importance of performance accountability and argues for a powerful prescription: "Budgeting is one of the most potent ways of introducing performance accountability into an organization . . . today, there's a built-in incentive to waste money. . . . [I'd recommend] drastically reducing the number of line items in an agency budget and allowing agencies to keep half of what they do not spend in any fiscal year. Give them a 'bucket' of money and hold them accountable for results" (Posner and Rothstein, 1994, p. 135).

## Consequences

Public organizations lack a bottom line comparable to the financial pressures and incentives that motivate private sector organizations. That, however, increases the urgency of using the budget system to ensure consequences.

In government, the budget system must help ensure that good performance is rewarded and that poor performers are identified with a process set in motion to repair the problems. Linking budget decisions to a performance measurement system will create a more effective system of incentives.

## Flexibility

By establishing performance accountability and consequences, essential preconditions are set to allow some authority over spending decisions to devolve from centralized, rule-bound control to other levels of the organization that are responsible for getting the job done right. With performance targets and resource parameters set, the budgeting system for high-performance public organizations must allow for greater flexibility to enable—even encourage—innovation and experimentation. Midlevel managers and front-line staff can be in a better position to decide how best to combine the "factors of production" to meet a set of continuously evolving challenges.

## Longer Time Frame

The overwhelming majority of local governments operate on annual budgets. States allocate, at best, on a two-year cycle. Although multiple-year projections are made on the federal level, the most important decisions are usually made in appropriations legislation that covers only a single year.

## Strategic Insights

Complexity, a paucity of information, and goals and objectives that are difficult to integrate are common characteristics of many of the issues or problems public agencies confront in carrying out their missions. The budget process should be enlisted to help develop strategic insights into the who, what, where, and how of government operations.

> *Who?* For example, which of the organizations we contract with to provide literacy training programs are best at reaching poor rural families and helping both parents and their children master essential skills?
>
> *What?* Should we, for example, increase funding for prenatal care through Medicaid or expand education and health services in the schools and through other local groups to dampen the growth in pregnancies among teenagers?
>
> *Where?* Are we investing the limited funding available for improving park facilities equitably, that is, where minority, disabled, and other traditionally underserved populations can access them?
>
> *How?* What are the key elements of successful programs that are helping welfare recipients progress from dependence to greater self-reliance?

By generating the information and insights we need to improve our understanding of the problems and consequences of alternative courses of action, budgeting systems play a central role in improving performance.

Effectively achieving public policy goals requires experimentation, continuous improvement, and an ability to learn over time. The budget systems can contribute to all three objectives.

## ALTERNATIVE BUDGET SYSTEMS FOR HIGH-PERFORMANCE ORGANIZATIONS

Budgeting practices are as varied as the range of public agencies, budget managers, and jurisdictions they serve. In thinking through the changes we need to make in our public sector budgeting systems to support high performance, it is helpful to review more traditional and alternative budgeting systems against the four criteria discussed earlier—accountability, consequences, flexibility, and strategic in-sights—as well as the strengths and weaknesses of each approach. These budgeting systems are *line item budgeting, performance budget-ing*, and *investment budgeting*.

## LINE ITEM BUDGETING: THE CONTROL ORIENTATION

"Line-item incremental budgeting is the process of making resource allocation decisions based on categories of spending, such as person-nel, equipment, etc." (Brizius, 1994, p. 4).

An early approach to budgeting, "the line-item or object of expen-diture budget is still the most common form found in most local gov-ernments" (Miller, 1992, p. 229). Under the line item budget, funds are allocated to very specific items or objects such as salaries, office supplies, or printing costs estimated for the next fiscal year (see Exhibit 9.2).

Under the line item budgeting system, the budget of even the largest agency is the sum total of such individual line items as they are set to cover (for example, personnel and benefit costs, expenses for supplies and new equipment, and the amount to be spent on food stamp benefits for eligible applicants over the next year).

### Strengths of Line Item Budgeting

The line item budget provides a high degree of fiscal and administra-tive control. Public agencies are held accountable for expenditures, as measured against an item-by-item spending schedule. Authority or control for setting these schedules is usually shared between the exec-utive and legislative branches. Generally, the system also provides for extensive involvement and oversight by central budget agencies and agency budget offices. Auditing and monitoring are relatively straight-

| | |
|---|---|
| Performance accountability | Poor |
| Consequences | Poor |
| Flexibility | Very limited |
| Strategic insights | Poor |

Exhibit 9.2.    Assessing the Line Item Budget.

forward; they focus on enforcing the expenditure limits and ensuring that resources are only expended on the limited purpose for which they are expressly appropriated.

## Limitations of Line Item Budgeting

Although line item budgeting is widely used and provides a high level of centralized control, it has very limited utility as a management tool (Miller, 1992).

First, it lacks flexibility. Precisely because the use of resources is so carefully limited by object of expenditure, unanticipated developments such as higher-than-average snowfall clogging the streets, an influx of immigrants requiring medical care, or a dip in the economy prompting a rapid rise in unemployment claims very often knock the most carefully crafted plans off the mark.

In addition, the allocation of funds among items tends to track closely with the patterns set in prior budgets. As such, your effort to adopt new approaches that necessitate a departure from the "traditional levels" can be thwarted by the system.

For example, some investments in telecommunications and information technology can both improve service and reduce costs. The fight to win a shift in spending authority to implement these changes, however, will often exceed the endurance of the champions of innovation.

Second, this system fails to relate the proposed line item estimates to performance against our policy objectives. The task of preparing budget proposals and evaluating them, setting expenditure levels and carrying them through, is plagued in practice by a paucity of information relating expenditures to accomplishments.

For example, a line item budget request might include detailed data on the number of teachers and the amount expended for education and training of the residents of the state juvenile corrections facility. However, proposed expenditures are not gauged against the outcomes we care about. The line item budget request is unlikely to provide useful information on results that count, such as improvement in reading skills, achievement of vocational competencies, or completion of General Equivalency Diploma (GED) programs by inmates. Policymakers are likely to be stymied in choosing how to best deploy the available resources. The detail and control orientation of the line item budget can hinder the ability of public leaders and agencies to make good on the promise of improved performance.

A third common flaw of the line item budget reflects the difficulty of integrating planning, policy development, budgeting, and fiscal or administrative control. Line item budgeting may reflect an implicit policy decision such as improving the job prospects of troubled youthful offenders. But getting better performance against that goal is difficult under the line item approach. Even though much detailed information on the cost of the inputs under the existing programs is available, the information needed to assess alternatives to the current approach is often lacking.

The best-laid plans of policy innovators are too often dashed on the rocks of a budget system tied to the past. Initiative becomes problematic, while inertia is promoted. Levels of service, organizational structure, and methods of operation become permanent, although they may be unsatisfactory.

## PERFORMANCE BUDGETING: THE MANAGEMENT APPROACH

"Performance budgeting is the process of making resource allocation decisions based on the achievement of measurable outcomes. It is also known as outcome-based budgeting" (Brizius, 1994, p. 4).

Reflecting the increase in activities and expenditures associated with implementing the New Deal, a form of performance budgeting was adopted by the federal government in the early 1930s. It differs from line item budgeting primarily in its orientation (see Exhibit 9.3). "Performance budgeting focuses attention on functions, activities, and projects rather than on single line-item components of a program" (Miller, 1992, p. 231). In tandem with the growing interest in program performance, these systems also introduced operational analysis, that is, methods for measuring inputs such as personnel and contractual services against outputs.

| | |
|---|---|
| Performance accountability | Improved |
| Consequences | Better, but stronger in theory than in practice |
| Flexibility | Improved |
| Strategic insights | Somewhat improved |

Exhibit 9.3.    Assessing Performance Budgeting.

Performance budget processes treat the budget much like a performance contract between an agency and the elected decision makers. The agency and elected leaders choose outcome measures in advance and agree to monitor performance. In return, agencies get greater leeway in spending money.

For example, after setting performance goals for the education and training program at the state's juvenile corrections facilities, executive and legislative branch budgeteers may settle on a single appropriation for the overall program for the coming year—with no line items or only two or three spending categories.

## Strengths of Performance Budgeting

Far and away the greatest advantage of this approach is the flexibility it can provide to those seeking to improve agency and policy performance. The basis for increased latitude to allocate resources to their highest possible return is the shift in orientation of the system away from bean counting and toward performance. Agency heads, bureau chiefs, supervisors, and front-line employees are challenged to examine more closely what they are accomplishing and how well their operations are performing.

Under performance budgeting, there is greater likelihood that the people who are best positioned to improve performance will be held more strictly accountable for what counts, such as educational attainment, rather than for what can be the most directly counted. An example of the latter type is whether the appropriation for textbooks was fully expended but not exceeded.

Good information cannot ensure good policy decisions. But it can help reduce the number of bad or poor decisions made because policymakers are in the dark. Although performance budgets require much more information to implement, they also yield much more of the kind of information needed to make better policy and program choices. Officials developing the budget must array information that details how many "outcomes" the state can afford. Elected leaders must choose among competing priorities. Agency personnel must achieve the performance targets, keeping close track of the unit cost of results (see Exhibit 9.4).

A principle thrust of performance budgeting is toward helping administrators assess operational performance against important policy goals. "It generates valuable data on the work efficiency of operating

The National Oceanic and Atmospheric Administration (NOAA) began to create a comprehensive strategic plan to improve performance and integrate performance management into agency budgeting shortly after new top leadership was appointed in 1993. In part, the agency's new leadership was seeking to end the "jelly bean problem." NOAA has traditionally had a large number of budget earmarks and a long list of individual budget lines. As a result, the agency operated more like five separate entities. The agency was also plagued by a lack of agreement on its mission or vision.

The first draft of a strategic plan for NOAA was developed internally within ninety days. It was refined through review with agency field staff and with a wide range of agency customers. The plan adopted seven goals that are applied agencywide. Each goal extended across the responsibilities of more than one line office. This change in framework helped move staff out of an office- or program-centered stove-pipe mentality. For example, tracking El Niño affects both short-term and long-term weather predictions, involves satellite monitoring, engages research staff, and affects efforts to manage fisheries.

Building from the seven goals, the agency was challenged to define objectives to support those goals. And they developed outcomes that would be the basis for the agency's first-time-ever effort at performance measurement. The effort included completing five-year implementation plans and single-year operating plans that are the basis of agency management.

Development of NOAA's budget is explicitly and consistently tied to the strategic plan. "If it's not in the plan, it's not funded," according to agency officials. NOAA changed the format and structure of the agency's budget to reduce programmatic silos and to present proposals in the context of the strategic goals. Those changes, however, have encountered some resistance from both the U.S. Office of Management and Budget and congressional committees. As a result, the agency produces two budgets. A traditional one is submitted to OMB and Congress. And a budget with the revised, more results-oriented format tied to the strategic goals is used within the agency. Some factors supporting NOAA's transition to strategic planning and a new approach to budgeting included the following:

1. The consistent interest and support from the agency's senior leadership included the commitment to building the strategic plan and to managing by it.

2. Early success helped build support. A key to getting buy-in from within the agency was the important role the strategic plan and planning cycle played with both OMB and Congress. The plan helped OMB understand for the first time what NOAA as an integrated agency is doing. That helped win approval for a budget increase in the president's budget proposal.

3. Integration of the strategic plan into the major management and policy cycles of the agency helped promote alignment to the plan's seven goals. For example, research, which is about 25 percent of NOAA, did not take the process seriously initially and, as a result, some significant programs were not funded. NOAA's field and lab directors were unhappy with that result and became a force for focusing more attention on doing it right.

4. Evaluation and incentive systems are also linked to the strategic plan. Incentives help focus senior managers. Fifty percent of the performance plans of senior managers are based on implementation and progress toward the goals.

5. The planners who created the strategic plan avoided developing reorganization proposals. Reorganization was viewed as likely to produce too much turmoil, consume too much energy, and leave too many of the old problems in place.

**Exhibit 9.4.  NOAA Integrates Strategic Plan and Performance Budgeting.**
*Source:* Fruchter, 1995.

units, casts budget categories in functional terms, and provides work-cost measurements to facilitate improving the performance" (Miller, 1992, p. 232).

## Limitations of Performance Budgeting

As with the case of its predecessor, performance budgeting is also often hampered by a short-term perspective. Most systems focus on the next year or, at best, the next two fiscal years.

In practice, budget estimates under this system are often no more meaningful than in line item budgets. This system does not go far enough in providing the rationale or criteria for choosing one expenditure plan over the other. Performance budgeting provides better information about policy and program outcomes. But as Brizius (1994) suggests, "It lacks the tools for comparing alternative spending plans and determining which will produce the most value" (p. 31).

## INVESTMENT BUDGETING

"Investment budgeting is designed to help improve the quality of resource allocation decisions by clarifying which options will yield a high return in the long run. . . . With better information, public leaders can make better choices among competing budget priorities and manage toward measurable results" (Brizius, 1994, p. 5).

Businesses rely on the predicted rate of return to choose between investment alternatives. Investment budgeting brings tools honed by the private sector to bear on improving the effectiveness of resource allocation decisions in government (see Exhibit 9.5).

Like performance budgeting, investment budgeting defines the outcomes to be achieved by public sector services and programs and

| | |
|---|---|
| Performance accountability | Improved |
| Consequences | Likely to be improved; long-term focus should be helpful |
| Flexibility | Improved |
| Strategic insights | Significantly improved, particularly with long-term focus and improved linkage between vision–mission statement and detailed information on program performance against policy goals |

**Exhibit 9.5.    Assessing Investment Budgeting.**

measures the cost of providing them under alternative strategies and spending levels. Investment budgeting goes beyond traditional systems, however, in gauging the value of the outcomes achieved. By establishing measurable outcomes and assessing both the costs and benefits of achieving them (the net present value), budget decisions made by government can also be guided by information on rates of return (see Exhibit 9.6).

## Strengths of Investment Budgeting

The tools used in investment budgeting are designed to support efforts to continuously improve performance. "Through the application of these tools, the problems and opportunities the public expects government to confront can be clarified, and a more rigorous process can be unleashed to identify more effective ways of addressing them" (Brizius, 1994, p. 8). Investment options that promise better rates of return will challenge the status quo, that is, the entrenched spending patterns and the interests that defend them.

Linking performance measurement to the monetary value placed on outcomes achieved is also a key to accountability. The service delivery system, at all levels, will face incentives to focus on activities that make the greatest progress toward achieving priority outcomes and to constantly seek innovations to improve their performance. In this way, investment budgeting helps ensure that effective performance is rewarded and that poor performers face appropriate consequences.

Investment decision making can also improve citizen participation in government. An open and public process to set priorities, define desirable goals, and specify measurable results is a prerequisite of investment budgeting. In addition, the results of public investments are

---

*Return on Investment:* The degree to which benefits exceed costs. It is expressed as a percentage per year.

*Value of Outcomes:* The value in monetary terms to individuals, government, and society as a whole of achieving desired outcomes.

*Net Present Value:* The value of a series of benefits or costs over time expressed in current dollars.

---

**Exhibit 9.6.    Investment Budgeting Key Definitions.**

*Source:* Brizius, 1994, pp. 27, 37–39.

reported against a consistent yardstick that can aid the press and the public in seeing where government is working and how investments improve people's lives and strengthen our communities (see Exhibit 9.7).

## Limitations of Investment Budgeting

Investment budgeting is more information-intensive than other budgeting systems. As with any complex system, it is likely to be only as strong as its weakest component. Doing it well entails a notable commitment of time and energy that must be sustained over the long term.

Quantifying the outcomes achieved by public sector investments is a second challenge. To do so, two estimates must be made: (1) a projection of what would happen in the future in the absence of action and (2) an estimate of the outcomes achieved that are attributable to the public sector's investment (see Exhibit 9.8).

Because the issues engaged by government are so complex and influenced by so many factors, experts are likely to reach divergent conclusions on these questions. Investment decision making will be difficult to implement without reaching consensus on these estimates. In addition, predicting outcomes achieved by new or innovative programs in which evaluation data are sparse or nonexistent may be particularly

| | |
|---|---|
| Maintenance Savings | |
| AFDC | $57,364,877 |
| Medicaid | 68,837,852 |
| Food stamp | 42,531,124 |
| Remediation/Public Protection Savings | |
| Children and youth services | 41,770,459 |
| Jail | 19,179,360 |
| Prison | 52,945,422 |
| Juvenile justice | 15,617,448 |
| Additional Revenues | 265,031,058 |
| Total | $563,277,600 |

**Exhibit 9.7.   Example Calculation of Savings from Investment in Improved Child and Family Well-Being in High-Risk Allegheny County Neighborhoods.**

*Source:* Bruner, Scott, and Stekette, 1996, p. 73.

---

In 1993, the Iowa legislature created the bipartisan Council on Human Investment (CHI) to develop and implement a system of performance management and investment budgeting for the state. Council initiatives include establishing state benchmarks, establishing an extensive process of public input, setting results-based performance measures for programs, and creating new results-based and investment budgeting models.

Iowa's efforts at budgeting for results links resource allocation, performance measurement, and policymaking. And it provides cost of a unit of performance (results) in order to support improved investment decision making. The model was implemented in selected agencies in fiscal year 1997. As a result, it is creating new opportunities for the legislature and state agencies to exchange greater flexibility for greater accountability for results. Governor Terry Branstad's goal is to implement budgeting for results in all agencies and programs by state fiscal year 2000.

The investment budget model is based on determining measurable results expected from services provided, determining the net present value of these results, creating a competitive marketplace for service delivery, and assessing and comparing return on investment from different strategies. CHI sees this model as leading to a greater focus on results of strategies rather than costs alone. Iowa is testing the system through a pilot effort in workforce development. The pilot, launched first in 1995, requires bidders to include a clear estimate of both the cost and return of identified outcomes. In exchange, the state grants more flexibility in program administration to participating service delivery areas.

---

**Exhibit 9.8.    Performance Management and Investment Budgeting in Iowa.**
*Sources:* Schilder, Brady, and Horsch, 1996, p. 36; Widner, 1996; Rosenberg, 1994.

---

contentious. If that proves to be the case, the lack of information and supporting analysis may well dampen the climate for innovation.

Setting monetary values on outcomes raises another set of difficulties. The perspective taken and the time frame used will drive results. Agreeing on the boundaries for making this calculation may be difficult. If the objective is to help move a family from welfare to self-sufficiency, for example, estimating the first-order effects (avoiding welfare, medical assistance, and housing costs) may be relatively easy. Second-order effects (the taxes that will be paid on future earnings) will be more difficult to attribute to a specific program or investment. Third-order effects may be important but very difficult to specify. Can cost savings in education, criminal justice, and job training programs be counted? Comparisons of expected rates of return on alternative investments will only be useful if the depth of analysis and other key assumptions are consistent.

# CHAPTER TEN

# High-Performance Human Resource Systems

he most difficult way to make productivity gains is to develop each worker's desire and ability to be maximally productive. But it is also the most enduring way to do so. The reason is simple. The people, in the long term, control the productivity of the organization.

The increasingly important role that human resource policies play in supporting high performance is being recognized by public and private organizations around the world (National Academy of Public Administration, 1995a). Aligning the overall values of the organization and the values expressed in human resource management (HRM) is a key step toward marshaling an organization's most important asset—the people who do the work and make the decisions—to achieve high performance. The values of the organization set the framework, and HRM policies and systems should reflect those values and put them into practice.

As NAPA concluded, "The HRM component of an organization—properly defined and implemented—can become a major value-adding element that contributes to achievement and results" (National Academy of Public Administration, 1995b, p. 9). Frank Cipolla, an innovative HRM policymaker during his tenure at the U.S. Department of Defense, stresses getting the organizational values right first. The overall organization should support the development of commitment, trust, and equity and place greater value on creativity, risk taking, involvement, responsibility, and achievement. Key values that HRM should emphasize include

*Competence.* Employees must have the knowledge, skills, and other characteristics necessary to perform their jobs at the highest levels of productivity and quality.

*Growth.* Training and on-the-job experiences should continuously build the capacities of employees throughout the organization.

*Equity.* All employees must be treated fairly and compassionately.

*Flexibility.* One-size-fits-all rules and systems do not reflect the realities of today's public employees or workplaces. Rigid rules hamper the adjustments necessary to respond to varied and changing circumstances.

*Diversity.* Diversity is essential to achieving organizational results.

*Accountability.* Individuals and groups must be properly supported before we move to hold them accountable for meeting current and high-performance goals.

Creating human resource policies that reinforce these values requires thinking in new ways about the people who work in our organizations. Employees are the preeminent asset, not components of a machine. HRM in high-performance companies or public agencies is not primarily about controlling labor costs; it is a value-adding component of the overall organization.

The private sector is learning these lessons. Applebaum and Batt (1994) find that HRM and industrial policies in companies that have won the prestigious Baldrige Award differ significantly from those in more conventionally managed companies. Award winners are more selective in hiring. Their investment in training in quality, group process, and job skills is higher. Employee pay is more closely tied to performance. And management and labor unions have forged new, more cooperative relationships.

Adopting a new line on HRM is adding to companies' bottom lines. Kravetz (1988) reports that a study of over seven hundred publicly held firms demonstrates a connection between human resource policies and performance. Progressive companies generally exhibited superior performance—higher sales per worker, lower employee turnover, improved gross profits, and better return to stockholders.

That lesson has been adopted by leaders in the private sector. John Welch Jr., chairman and chief executive of General Electric, describes his approach this way. "We would not knowingly hire anyone in our company that was not 'boundaryless,' that was not open to an idea from anywhere, that was not excited about a learning environment" (Chapman-Welch, 1997, p. H1).

Governments at all levels face enormous challenges of rapidly changing economic and social systems. In this time of change, the public sector needs leadership that is responsive and agencies that can effectively draw on limited resources to meet the changing needs of the American people. Revamping HRM policies and practices can clear away roadblocks and unclog organizational arteries. If we do so, our public agencies will be better positioned to attract and keep the people with the energy, talent, and commitment needed to succeed. And we are unlikely to achieve high performance unless we do so.

## CHARACTERISTICS OF HIGH-PERFORMANCE HUMAN RESOURCE POLICIES AND PRACTICES

A comprehensive study by NAPA of innovative HRM practices (National Academy of Public Administration, 1995b) and the efforts of the National Performance Review (National Performance Review, 1993) suggest principles to guide reform of federal HRM policies. These principles, applicable across the public sector, include the following:

High-performance organizations adopt flexible and adaptable HRM policies and practices through deregulation and simplification.

Authority is more decentralized and delegated to the lowest practical level. Executives and managers are responsible and accountable for managing people.

Organizational goals and values are reinforced through incentives and accountability systems.

HRM policies are responsive to the changing workforce and workplace.

New collaborative relationships between employees, unions, and management are created to facilitate change and employee participation.

The organization and its employees invest in building competency and human capital.

HRM is integrated into the development and implementation of overall organizational strategic plans.

The role of HRM professionals shifts from reactive paper processors to more of a partner, consultant, and change agent. HRM is measured by and accountable for its contribution to the organization's mission.

## STRATEGIES FOR MOVING TOWARD HIGH-PERFORMANCE HUMAN RESOURCE MANAGEMENT

There are a wide array of HRM policies and practices that hold promise for helping our organizations reach high performance. Many have been tested and have demonstrated their value.

### Simplify Job Classifications

The federal classification system, with 459 job series, fifteen grades, and ten steps within grades, did not work. As the NPR concluded, it had become too time consuming, expensive, cumbersome, and intensely frustrating to allow it to remain unreformed (National Performance Review, 1993).

State and local governments are often plagued by a similar blizzard of complexity. In states, for example, the number of job classifications ranges from a low of 551 in South Dakota to as high as 7,300 in New York. In too many state and local governments, these systems are so "rule-bound and complicated that merit is often the last value served" (National Commission on the State and Local Public Service, 1993, pp. 24–25, 27).

Created to prevent abuses and to promote fairness, centralization of authority and prescriptive rules in HRM have "grown to the point where managers do not have the tools they need to manage effectively—the authority to hire, reward, and sanction" (National Performance Review, 1993, p. 13).

The direct costs, such as cost of the staff in the HRM bureaucracy and other staff, are burdensome. The indirect costs imposed through the dampening effect some systems have on performance, such as limiting the ability to better match job assignments with shifting needs, are inestimable.

Both the private and public sectors, according to NAPA (National Academy of Public Administration, 1991), are adopting a modernized classification system—broad banding. "Under broad banding, several occupations are grouped together into families or career paths. Through this approach the number of job classifications and pay ranges is cut sharply" (National Academy of Public Administration, 1994, p. 4).

## Streamline and Improve Recruitment and Selection

As conditions and needs change, public agencies need to overhaul recruitment strategies. Many public employers rely mainly on passive recruitment methods. In an age when the public sector must compete vigorously for the best talent available, finding and hiring the best possible new employees requires more attention.

Our agencies need to use more aggressive outreach, particularly to groups underrepresented in the existing workforce. Creating comprehensive recruitment plans will help to clearly define current and future personnel needs and to identify likely sources for people with these skills.

Excessive reliance on written tests and outdated procedures are problems in some public sector hiring systems. A careful assessment should determine whether testing procedures currently in use are biased, out-of-date, or poor predictors of competency and performance. Revising tests and testing practices can make them more job-related. Some agencies find that adding selection criteria other than written tests is critical to finding and promoting good people.

Zone scoring or broad banding is another alternative. In zone scoring, candidates are given scores of A, B, and C rather than specific numerical scores. These changes would open interviews to more candidates and allow more weight to be placed on factors other than test performance.

Some public sector employers limit the number of candidates who can be considered in the interviewing process. Restrictive rules include the "rule of three" and other eligibility certification provisions. Rigid formal education and experience requirements could also be reduced or eliminated. When these types of inflexible rules are reformed, agencies and managers can consider a larger number of qualified job seekers (see Exhibit 10.1).

Across government we can also look within to meet our needs. Expanded training programs can help prepare existing employees to fill new staffing needs or move into more challenging positions.

Finally, some HRM experts recommend adopting entry-level or contingent employment status for employees entering the workforce. To do so would deemphasize testing prior to hiring and increase the focus on observed performance in determining merit and competence.

## Decentralize and Delegate HRM Authority

As line managers are held more accountable for improved productivity, they need greater control over human resources. We can and should reform HRM practices to give managers a stronger voice in the selection, compensation, training, promotion, and separation of employees.

Both the NPR and the Winter Commission recommend substantial decentralization of many HRM functions, with more authority for

---

A U.S. Department of Agriculture demonstration project tested alternative recruitment systems at 140 experimental and 80 comparison locations nationwide (National Performance Review, 1993, p. 12). Test sites used a streamlined, agency-based recruitment and hiring process rather than the Office of Personnel Management's centralized system. Recruitment incentives were available, and the probationary period for research scientists was extended. An independent evaluation by Pennsylvania State University documented the benefits:

- Increased access to local labor markets
- Greater control over the hiring process
- Better-quality applicants in the candidate pool
- Improved public perceptions of the agency as an employer and community member
- Strong preference by participating sites for the more flexible system over central listings and registers

The streamlined and more flexible alternative has now become policy. All federal agencies now have essentially this authority.

---

**Exhibit 10.1.   USDA Tests Alternative Hiring Strategies.**

personnel-related decisions delegated to line managers. Under this approach, agencies and line managers conduct their own recruiting and examining for all positions and have greater decision-making authority on position classification, pay, and employee evaluation (National Academy of Public Administration, 1993).

Extending more HRM responsibility to line managers is an accepted principle in the private sector. NAPA (National Academy of Public Administration, 1995a) found that AT&T, Hewlett-Packard, Intel, and Xerox already use this approach. And, as seen in Exhibit 10.2, some governments are following suit (National Academy of Public Administration, 1995a). In Oregon's Multnomah County, for example, managers make hiring decisions, ensure that their employees are paid at the proper rates, and carry out performance assessments. Under the county's continuous improvement initiative, managers spend less time monitoring daily work, which frees them to do more planning.

Strategies for facilitating the transfer of more HRM authority to line managers include

Simplifying HRM policies and systems

Using information technology to ease paperwork burdens

Training managers in new skills and supporting them with consulting services

Setting a limited number of clear goals that align with organizational mission

Addressing resistance to risk taking and other changes in organizational culture

---

Civil service reforms in the state of Washington include a separate system—Washington Management Service (WMS)—for approximately two thousand managers (NAPA, 1995a, p. 99). WMS administration is more decentralized, with line managers exercising greater authority to hire, classify, and evaluate employees without involvement of the Department of Personnel. Other features include

- Broad banding to cut the number of job classifications by 350
- More flexibility to set and change salaries
- Due process protections to ensure that managers are only dismissed, suspended, or demoted for cause

---

**Exhibit 10.2.  Washington Management Service.**

## Hold Managers Accountable
## for Human Resource Management

Where authority is delegated to front-line managers, our performance goals and evaluation processes should reinforce the importance of attending to HRM problems and opportunities. The evaluation of line managers in leading companies is based on their contribution to business success, customer satisfaction, and their efforts to build the organization's human capacity (National Academy of Public Administration, 1995b). Measures include surveys of employees and 360-degree appraisal systems, with ratings linked to rewards and sanctions.

Managers also need training to prepare them to assume new HRM responsibilities. "Training needs are likely to include: personnel system operation; teamwork processes; business management skills; problem solving techniques; communication techniques; and leadership/motivation" (National Academy of Public Administration, 1995b, p. 37).

## Reinforce Organizational Goals and Values

Compensation policies such as gainsharing and more closely linking pay to performance will help reinforce organizational goals and values.

*Gainsharing increases incentives for high performance.* Under gainsharing, some of the savings from productivity improvements or other innovations fund cash bonuses, pay increases, or other non-pay benefits. Gainsharing is a powerful incentive for all employees to work together to identify barriers to performance and to develop new approaches to overcome them.

Where they have been implemented, gainsharing policies boast some impressive improvements in performance. "A study of private sector firms with gainsharing plans in place for more than five years shows the companies saved an average of 29 percent in labor costs" (U.S. General Accounting Office, 1996, p. 33). Comparable savings, as well as improvements in employee participation and labor-management relationships, can be found in the public sector (National Academy of Public Administration, 1994).

*Compensation for public employees must be comparable to the private sector.* Public dissatisfaction with government and ongoing fiscal pressures severely strain the ability of many governments to keep compensation levels on a par with the private sector. Narrowing these gaps will help clear an important hurdle from the path to high performance in public agencies.

*Compensation should be more closely tied to performance.* Pay for performance "includes a number of approaches that more closely tie employee pay to performance appraisals or accomplishments against specific goals" (American Federation of Labor-Congress of Industrial Organizations, 1991, p. 23). These include group incentive plans, gain-sharing, pay banding, career development pay, and variable pay (see Exhibit 10.3).

However, at least one review of pay-for-performance schemes in state and local governments concluded that the systems promise more than they deliver (Narcisso, 1996). The study suggests three areas for reform that can help improve the effectiveness of pay-for-performance systems. These include increasing funding, reducing complexity, and improving evaluation systems and administrative processes.

*Employee appraisal and incentives policies must be improved.* Good performance appraisal systems facilitate information exchange between managers and employees and influence future performance and work motivation. However, public sector job evaluation schemes too often focus on process rather than results.

Morhman, Resnick-West, and Lawler (1990) found that the lack of specific and realistic individual goals and good measurement methods also hamper effective appraisal processes for many public employees. The appraisal process should integrate the organization's goals for change and improvement with the criteria used to evaluate employee performance. We need to place greater emphasis on each employee's contribution to achieving our organization's overall mission and objectives.

---

Jacksonville, Florida, gives performance-based bonuses to reward city employees through three performance measurement systems (Mohrman, Resnick-West, and Lawler, 1990, p. 5). For the past thirteen years, the city has used an employee evaluation system covering six thousand civil servants. Supervisors set job factors unique to each position, rate employees annually, and usually give merit raises of 5 percent to two or three people within a division. The merit incentive system and a special goals and objectives program covers three hundred employees (mostly managers) and offers a combined 3 to 8 percent boost. Through the three systems, Jacksonville has made productivity a personal issue for employees.

---

Exhibit 10.3.   Productivity Rewards for Jacksonville Employees.

Effective appraisal systems are difficult to develop, implement, and sustain. The potential benefits from improving employee appraisal and incentive systems, however, merit the time and attention necessary to redesign them. Including a larger cross-section of the organization in the process of reforming appraisal systems—front-line employees, middle managers, and top officials in addition to human resource management professionals—is a good first step.

*Non-pay incentives can provide effective rewards.* Most reward systems focus on financial rewards. These are not the only (or necessarily the most important) rewards for many employees. Other inducements include

Pruning back rules and regulations affecting the employee

Cutting or easing day-to-day paperwork, interruptions, and administrative tasks

Allowing employees time and funds to further their career development goals

Providing greater freedom of choice of assignments

Offering flexible deadlines and working hours

Delegating responsibilities and relying more on employees' judgment and discretion

*Employees should be rewarded for improving their skills and job-related competencies.* Government employers and employees can work together to define basic and more advanced skills needed to perform specific job groupings. Financial awards, pay raises, and non-pay incentives should be explicitly linked to demonstrating mastery of those skills.

*Incentives should reinforce successful team builders.* Most evaluations focus on individual performance. Some public agencies, however, factor measures of group performance into individual performance appraisals. Appraisals for the management team at National Aviation Supply Office in Philadelphia recognize individual contributions but emphasize team performance. First, standards used to rate individual performance are identified. Next, top management assesses the team's accomplishment of its corporate strategies to determine the team's rating. Supervisors then compare individual accomplishments on common team elements to the organization's overall rating. Finally, "ratings of record" combine both the individual's and the organization's performance rating.

# RESPONSIVE HRM POLICIES

High-performance organizations are responsive to the changing nature of the workforce and workplace. Long-range trends are changing the makeup of the workforce, raising new issues that the private and public sectors must address.

Trends identified by Johnson, Faul, Huang, and Packer (1988) include

> *An aging workforce.* The number of people aged forty-eight through fifty-three will increase by 67 percent by the turn of the century.
>
> *Increased diversity.* Women now make up 45 percent of the workforce. As of 1990, 65 percent of all women with children were employed for pay. The percentage of the workforce that is nonwhite has grown from 11 percent in 1970 to 14 percent by 1985 and is likely to reach 16 percent by 2000.
>
> *A changing mix of family and household structures.* The traditional structure—male breadwinner, female helpmate, and 2.5 children—now accounts for only 15 percent of households. The number of single-headed and dual-earner households is growing rapidly. And dual-earner families will account for 90 percent of husband-wife families by 2000.

We can develop and adopt policies and practices to meet these changing needs. "In the 1990s, efforts to attract and retain the best possible employees to public service at the federal, state, and local levels will grow more challenging" (National Academy of Public Administration, 1993, p. xvii). In the past, many governments have been model employers. They have often led the way in adopting progressive personnel practices. That record must be sustained and built upon in the years ahead. Personnel policies for meeting changing workforce needs could include

Flexible and compressed work schedules

Expanded opportunities for part-time employment and position sharing

Greater availability of either paid or unpaid family and medical leave

Leave sharing to allow employees to donate unused leave days for use by others who have exhausted all their leave in meeting personal or family emergencies

Policies and equipment to facilitate telecommuting and work-at-home programs (using satellite work centers is another approach being developed by both private and public employers)

More available and affordable child and adult day care

Cafeteria-style benefit plans that provide employees with more flexibility to customize their own benefit packages

## NEW COLLABORATIVE RELATIONSHIPS

High-performance public organizations forge new partnerships among management, employees, and their union representatives. Public leaders are learning what many of their private sector counterparts already know: great changes in organizational culture and performance cannot be accomplished without great cooperation from employees and unions.

Just as employee involvement is vital to organizational change, labor-management relations are critical to employee involvement. Where cooperative labor-management relationships and participatory management models have been adopted, significant joint gains can be realized by management, employees, and unions. And unions, according to the International Personnel Management Association, Federal Section (1993), have been an asset to the change process, contributing new ideas and solutions, spreading high-performance systems, and building employee commitment and participation.

### New Labor-Management Structures Can Help Improve Performance

Labor and management can work together as more equal partners to develop more democratic and productive work environments. Constructive involvement of employees and their representatives is a key strategy in any attempt to increase performance in government.

John Sturdivant, as head of the seven-hundred-thousand-member American Federation of Government Employees, saw the need to change the relationship between AFGE and federal agency employers: "Over the past twelve years, federal unions defined a strategy of obstruction to a high degree of efficiency using a combination of negotiation, litigation, press leaks, and congressional oversight hearings. That is not what we wanted to do. This is the time for us to change the way we do business. It is time to step up and be part of the solution. Until federal employees can communicate to the American people that we are as concerned about creating a more efficient and effective government, we will always find ourselves under political attack" (Sturdivant, 1994). Sturdivant identifies six factors that have helped support efforts to strengthen labor-management cooperation and partnership.

Leadership—on both sides of the table

Open mindedness

Acceptance of the need to change and a desire to play a proactive role in shaping change

Mutual respect

Knowledge and training for both management and union officials on how to use new techniques

A base of communication leading to a less adversarial climate

High-performance organizations are shifting away from traditional, adversarial approaches to labor-management relationships. Partnerships between labor and management help ensure the free and open participation by employees and their representatives in decisions that affect their jobs.

Trust and commitment of all parties must be built for these new relationships to succeed. Changing the character of labor-management relationships involves creating the capacity for the parties to work with each other in a different framework and expanding the scope of the discussions beyond mandatory and permissive subjects to business and human issues that have the greatest effects on performance.

The formation of labor-management committees is one approach that appears to work. The State and Local Government Labor-Management Committee (1992, pp. 4–7), made up of twenty major public management and union organizations, lists some keys to creating more effective labor-management committees.

1. Top-level representatives from both labor and management are committed to the effort.

2. The process is cochaired by labor and management.

3. Committees set their own agendas and scope by identifying problems and issues of mutual concern for study and action.

4. The process encourages free sharing of a wide range of views and information.

5. Conclusions and recommendations are made only when consensus is achieved.

## New Approaches to Collective Bargaining and Conflict Resolution

In traditional labor-management negotiations, each side has its position, and the two sides negotiate for their respective bottom lines. One party wins and the other loses (or compromise means neither party completely meets its needs).

Alternatively, labor and management can bargain for mutual gain. Each still advocates its own interests. But, they also cooperate to look for solutions whereby the interests of both sides are met. Achieving win-win solutions can be difficult (see Exhibit 10.4). The problem-solving process can be the basis for continued improvement in working relationships on issues of shared concern.

---

The Hawaii Board of Education, State Teachers Association, and the Government Employees Association used "win-win" bargaining in negotiating their new contract in 1994. In the process, the new labor-management relationship is supporting real progress on educational reform (Popovich, 1994).

In contrast to a twenty-year history of generally contentious negotiations, the win-win process emphasized collaborative problem solving. For example, participants in the negotiations banished table pounding, name calling, and secret caucuses. Greater emphasis was placed on sharing information and developing new solutions to jointly defined problems.

Successes include

- The contracts were settled on time and without resorting to the intervention of outside mediation.
- The new agreement granted more flexibility at the school level that allows Hawaii to go further in implementing site-based school management.
- Retention bonuses were designed to reduce the turnover of principals and to encourage leadership stability that can support school reform.

---

**Exhibit 10.4.    Hawaii Gains from Win-Win Bargaining.**

Both public and private employers use alternative dispute resolution techniques to improve collective bargaining and grievance processes. Deemphasizing confrontation and adopting carefully structured joint processes to identify problems, share information, and develop more creative solutions can benefit both management and public employees. Alternative collective bargaining approaches such as win-win or interest-based bargaining are being demonstrated with success in negotiations between public employers and unions.

### Building the Capacity of Unions

A study of federal labor-management relations by the International Personnel Management Association, Federal Section (1993, p. 25), highlights the importance of union security to creating more cooperative relationships with management: "a healthy federal labor-management relationship requires a strong fiscal foundation to support vigorous, independent unions which fairly represent federal workers in dealings with employees."

Negotiating agency shop agreements is one approach to strengthening union partners. In an agency shop, all employees in the bargaining unit either join the union or pay a service fee. Employees are not required to join the union. However, their fees help to defray costs of negotiations, contract administration, and other services they receive from the union.

## INVEST IN BUILDING COMPETENCY AND HUMAN CAPITAL

High-performance organizations increase their investment in training to build their most important asset: human capital. Baldrige Award winners, for example, dedicate 10 percent or more of their payroll to training. The Australian government, which has been at government reform work longer than the United States, allocates 5 percent of personnel costs to education and training for public employees.

### Increase Investments in Human Capital

The public sector in the United States lags badly behind. During the 1980s, the federal government committed only about 1 percent of payroll to training. Investment in human-capital development must become a higher priority.

As a target, our agencies should aim for a stable "learning budget" of at least 3 percent of total personnel costs (National Performance Review, 1993, p. 78). To achieve this goal, we must make the case both internally and to outside stakeholders that expanded investments in employee training and development are crucial to reaching productivity and quality improvement goals.

The Bureau of Reclamation in the U.S. Department of Commerce, for example, is a proven leader in federal reinvention. In about two years, the bureau shifted its mission, decentralized decision making, and adopted plans to shrink its budget and staffing by 25 percent. To facilitate these changes, the bureau doubled its training and development budget (Maymi, 1995).

## Change the Focus and Delivery of Training

More funding is a necessary but insufficient step toward providing the training and educational programs needed for the future. Changes in focus and delivery mechanisms also merit consideration. For example, in a more competitive model, rather than putting all the available funding into the agency training office, funds are apportioned into individual employee training accounts. General guidelines help ensure that spending is consistent with the organization's mission. However, this approach empowers employees, rather than the training office, to decide what training they want and who they want to provide it.

## INTEGRATE HRM INTO THE DEVELOPMENT OF STRATEGIC PLANS

The private sector has moved aggressively to link HRM to strategic planning and align HRM with their goals and strategies (National Academy of Public Administration, 1995a). Just as mission and business objectives should drive HRM, HRM officials should be active participants when organizational plans, goals, and objectives are set.

We must strengthen the linkages between strategic planning and HRM as we seek high performance. As our mission and objectives are refined, all aspects of HRM should be assessed to determine whether it is effectively fulfilling its role of maintaining a high-quality public service that meets the goals for productivity, quality, and program results.

Integrating human resource issues into the budget planning process is a good starting place. Formal advisory committees, with participants drawn from the organization's top leaders, managers, employees, and employee representatives, can be given the task of assessing HRM performance and proposing refinements.

Among the states, Florida, Minnesota, North Carolina, and Oregon are leading the pack in better aligning HRM policies with organizational goals. All four states are implementing legislation mandating results-oriented management reforms. Florida encourages agencies to try new HRM ideas as pilot programs. Their new law allows waivers of both administrative and statutory requirements agencies believe are barriers to improving performance.

## THE SHIFTING ROLE OF HRM PROFESSIONALS

Where responsibility for HRM is shared with line managers, HRM should assist and advise them in using and adapting HRM programs, policies, and processes that advance the organization's objectives. Consultative duties focus on working alongside managers to address current business needs.

The shift will require new approaches to HRM, and HRM professionals must develop new skills. At the least, it will increase the need for generalists able and available to work "out front" where line managers operate (National Academy of Public Administration, 1995b). A focus group of federal managers, employees, and HRM specialists highlights skills needed by HRM staffs, as shown in Exhibit 10.5.

## HRM: MEASURING PERFORMANCE AND BUILDING ACCOUNTABILITY

Measurement and accountability are hallmarks of high-performance organizations. They are as important to reinventing HRM as dramatically improving production or service functions. Effectiveness and efficiency are key dimensions, and there is a range of methods to gauge progress toward organizational and HR goals (see Exhibit 10.6).

| Identified by Managers | Identified by Employees | Identified by HRM Specialists |
|---|---|---|
| Consulting skills | Mission knowledge | HR knowledge |
| Generalist HR knowledge | Knowledge of information technology | Communications skills |
| Line management orientation | Communications skills | Problem-solving skills |
| Analytical skills | Change management skills | Time management skills |
| Team process skills | Business skills | Knowledge of information technology |
| Customer focus | Risk taking | Total-quality-management skills |
| Planning skills | Generalist HR knowledge | Consulting skills |
| Knowledge of information technology | Team process skills | Systems approach |
| Flexibility | Work planning and prioritization skills | Innovation |
| Innovation | People skills | |

**Exhibit 10.5.    Skills and Competencies Needs.**

*Source:* National Academy of Public Administration, 1995b, p. 37.

| What to Measure? | Measurements |
|---|---|
| Organizational Success | • Mission reviews and evaluations<br>• Surveys on satisfaction with and recommendations for HRM services<br>• Process cycle time<br>• Accuracy and rework rates |
| Efficiency | • Comparative costs and ratios with other like organizations<br>• Costs per employee serviced by subfunction<br>• Average salary and grade, sick leave rates, and injury compensation costs |
| Trend Data | • Volume of actions processed by subfunction<br>• Number of grievances, appeals, lawsuits, and disputes with employee unions<br>• Hiring and promotion rates by age, race, and ethnic group<br>• Average age/retirement eligibility<br>• Promotion rate/average years in grade |

**Exhibit 10.6.    Elements of an HRM Measurement System.**

*Source:* National Academy of Public Administration, 1995, adapted from Figure 6, pp. 37–39.

# High-Performance Procurement Systems

—∿—

Doing business with government, supplying the public sector's demand for goods and services, is big business. The federal government alone commits almost $200 billion annually (15 percent of the total budget) for goods and services (Friar and Leonard, 1994, p. 23). If procurement by all levels of government is included, spending reaches $450 billion each year. In fact, government's appetite for buying accounts for about 10 percent of the total U.S. gross national product (U.S. Department of Commerce, 1988, p. 60).

Although public procurement is big business, it has been a relatively quiescent field. Generally, these systems work well in administering an open and fair process that delivers the goods at a fair price. Neither the public, the agencies, nor elected officials focus much attention on procurement issues unless a scandal arises.

In recent years, procurement problems and outright dishonesty were uncovered at all levels of government. Multi-million-dollar overcharges on defense systems, kickback schemes on local construction projects, and inequitable treatment of small companies in awarding contracts are all examples of these problems. Front-page headlines often follow. And even when these abuses are exceptions, officials scramble to respond to shaken public confidence by imposing new controls and regulations as safeguards.

As a result, a cumbersome and time-consuming process has taken shape over the decades as the best way to protect taxpayer dollars. Public agencies and their suppliers are left to wrestle with a procurement system made more unwieldy through the accretion of piecemeal solutions.

The National Commission on State and Local Public Service concluded in 1993 that critical aspects of procurement laws, regulations, and operating procedures are not meeting important public purposes: "Procurement practices have become so complex and so expensive that many of our best companies refuse to bid on government contracts because it is simply not worth the time and effort. Government managers and employees, meanwhile, cannot obtain the supplies or equipment they need or cannot get them when they need them" (National Commission on the State and Local Public Service, 1993, p. 34).

The National Performance Review arrived at a similar conclusion: "The federal procurement system relies on rigid rules and procedures, extensive paperwork, detailed design specifications, and multiple inspections and audits. It is an extraordinary example of bureaucratic red tape. . . . Rules are changed too often and are so process-oriented that they minimize discretion and stifle innovation" (National Performance Review, 1993, pp. 26–28).

Indeed, the public trust demands an honest, fair, accountable, and open procurement system. These values must be maintained and strengthened through any revisions to public procurement processes. Taxpayers, however, deserve even more than that. Procurement practices must also support the creation of high-performance agencies that get the public's business done faster and better while delivering the best value.

## CHARACTERISTICS OF HIGH-PERFORMANCE PUBLIC PROCUREMENT SYSTEMS

Agencies and public leaders are taking steps to reform procurement systems to support the achievement of high-performance goals. Based on their innovations, we have identified eight steps you can consider in developing a reform agenda for your agency:

1. Emphasize quality and value in procurement decisions.

2. Increase discretion and flexibility in procurement decision making, and hold procurement systems more accountable for results.

3. Streamline paperwork and procurement processes.

4. Decentralize more responsibility for procurement processes and decisions.

5. Stress a service-oriented approach and the support functions of centralized purchasing agencies.

6. Support procurement improvements with training and opportunities to spread innovations.

7. Improve procurement protest, appeals, and conflict resolution processes.

8. Enhance enforcement against fraud and abuse in government procurement.

## Emphasize Quality and Value

Former astronaut John Glenn, recollecting the final minutes before the launch of his Mercury mission, confesses that he tried not to dwell on the idea that his rocket was the product of thousands of least-cost government contracts. For NASA, quality can be a life-or-death issue. The caliber of office equipment bought for the highway agency and the cleaning services contracted for public schools do not entail such peril. Quality and value, nevertheless, must be an expected "deliverable" in all public procurements (see Exhibit 11.1).

Generally, laws and regulations governing procurement do not prohibit officials from placing equal weight on quality and value vis-à-vis the lowest price. The culture that imbues purchasing decisions in public agencies, however, can militate against an increased emphasis on quality and value (Kelman, 1990). Both the "rapidly growing number of costly appeals of contracting choices and the tendency to stress 'objective data' in bid evaluations can cause a shift toward hard factors—such as price—and away from more difficult to quantify criteria—such as quality and value" (Kelman, 1990, p. 28).

Administrative changes adopted by procurement offices and amendments to public contracting laws are addressing concerns over the balance among cost and quality and value. "Systems stressing 'best

The purchase of information technology is among the most difficult contracting decisions confronting government agencies. In the fall of 1993, however, California codified "best value" as the criteria for evaluating data processing, telecommunications, and systems integration procurement. The new Value Effective Procurement (Johnson, 1994) sets criteria to be considered, including:

- Product quality
- Vendor's financial stability, prior performance, and experience with projects of similar scope and complexity
- Reliability of vendor's delivery and implementation schedules
- Extent of integration and data exchange with existing systems
- Warranties, guarantees, and return policy
- Operational costs incurred if the bid is accepted

Exhibit 11.1.    Value Is Job #1.

value' decisions specify that product quality, total life-cycle cost, risk associated with the procurement, and vendors' track records must be given equally or greater weight than low base price" (National Governors' Association, 1993, p. 53).

## Build Accountability

Increased flexibility and reliance on the professionalism and common sense of government procurement officers may be a key to improving system performance. "That does not mean handing anyone a blank check. It does mean empowering the people who make the system work and holding them accountable for achieving results" (Angle, 1994).

## Increase Flexibility

Over-reliance on layers of process safeguards creates procurement processes that are severely hamstrung. Kelman (1990) suggests that "depriving government officials of discretion that could produce misbehavior also limits the discretion that could call forth outstanding achievement" (p. 86).

Two major limitations on discretion in procurement through competitive bidding processes and alternative approaches aimed at increasing flexibility while promoting improved performance are reviewed next (see Exhibit 11.2).

The Federal Aviation Administration slashed procurement processing time by two-thirds or more (Hulick, 1995). Major purchases, which once took six years, are being completed in two years by using "Draft Requests for Proposals." The drafts enabled industry to give feedback before specifications are set. The result? The agency has saved time and has captured better, cheaper technical solutions by bringing bidders into the process earlier and using their ideas and technical expertise better. Another experiment—videotaped proposals—cut twelve months from an eighteen-month solicitation process and all but a few weeks from what had been a ten-month review period.

Exhibit 11.2.    FAA Takes Off with Procurement Reform.

## Establish RFP Requirements

"Painfully detailed specifications and carefully crafted contractual clauses have evolved as a primary avenue to guaranteeing quality and value in public procurement" (Kelman, 1990, p. 19). However, this traditional approach is becoming less effective as the nature of the goods and services government buys is changing. Simple and standard products are a shrinking portion of government's shopping list. The task of completing workable specifications and satisfactory contractual language, therefore, becomes increasingly problematic.

Making greater use of functional specifications instead of detailing technical specifications is one change adopted by some procurement agencies. With functional specifications, agencies outline their problem rather than preselect a "solution" to interested vendors. Businesses responding to the RFP, rather than the agency and its procurement office, have the widest latitude to apply their unique knowledge and expertise toward crafting innovative and cost-effective solutions.

## Evaluate Proposals from Vendors

Procurement laws and regulations allow considerable, but not unlimited, discretion in setting evaluation criteria. Requiring clarity and detailed specification of the methods and criteria to be used to evaluate proposals has advantages. The rigidity of that approach, however, also presents significant limitations.

First, procurement agencies tend to place the greatest emphasis on criteria that are most amenable to quantification. "Benefits to the agency that are hard to quantify tend to be excluded" (Kelman, 1990, p. 20). As a result, important but difficult-to-document benefits are given an inordinately low weight.

Second, "while procurement officials often have flexibility to indicate the relative importance of evaluation criteria, exact weighing factors are most common in public procurement" (Kelman, 1990, p. 56). Private companies, in sharp contrast, seldom use fixed evaluation weights in their procurement decisions. Leaving more discretion to decide on criteria and the specific weight each will be given until after proposals are received would allow new information learned by the agency or provided by potential vendors to play a greater role in procurement decision making.

Third, and potentially most perverse, are limits on the use in the procurement process of information likely to be useful in making contractor selection decisions. Because past contractor performance is considered too subjective by some procurement officials, for example, it is often ruled out of consideration. Even where RFPs require contractor-provided references, this information is often given little weight in evaluation. In the private sector, experience with contractors is an important factor in purchasing decisions (Kelman, 1990). The lack of emphasis on past contractor performance yields a perverse incentive. "Contractors who establish exemplary performance records, develop new solutions, and/or provide valuable preaward technical assistance receive little benefit for their efforts" (Kelman, 1990, p. 66). Nor are poor performers penalized.

### End Use-It-Or-Lose-It Rules

As the end of the fiscal year approaches, the flow of procurement requests in many public agencies rises to flood-tide levels. The countdown to close out is a rational response to an irrational rule; any funds budgeted for procurement that are not committed by the fiscal year's end are lost to the agency. As a result, there are few incentives for economizing on surplus funds. Alternatively, agencies could be granted general or limited authority to carry over unspent funds.

### Build Accountability

Equity, integrity, and efficiency are the traditional standards used to judge the performance of procurement systems. Critics of current practices note, however, that "contributing to excellence in the performance of the organization's substantive task is conspicuous by its absence from this list" (Kelman, 1990, p. 11).

Building an accountability system begins by identifying those roles and responsibilities of the procurement system that most directly influence progress toward the agency's core mission and objectives. This involves both scrutiny of the overall strategic plan and a careful audit of the entire procurement process.

Next, quantifiable goals are established and drive regular appraisals of both system performance and individual achievement. A commitment of top leadership to providing incentives to reward good performance and to targeting attention to areas that must be improved completes the key elements.

Setting process and service standards can be a valuable interim step in moving toward holding the system more responsible for yielding real results (see Exhibit 11.3). Examples of areas that should be considered include

Cutting the lag time between requisition and fulfillment

Improving service, as measured by satisfaction ratings from system customers and front-line managers and employees

Reducing grievances and appeals by bidders

## STREAMLINE PAPERWORK AND PROCESSES

It used to require written authorization from twenty-three people before a federal agency could buy a personal computer. Paperwork and multiple reviews also plague state and local procurement systems,

---

Improvements in systems and procedures at Washington state's Department of Labor and Industries slashed the time it takes to buy desktop computers from three months to less than nine days. Teams of customers, service providers, and information system procurement experts used techniques from business process reengineering to improve order fulfillment for personal computers. They revised the system by ranking business functions on a three-dimensional scale that evaluated customer satisfaction with the services, the services' importance to the organization, and the ability of the organization to improve those services. After the assessment, the agency collapsed eleven procurement processes down to two, revised procedures, sped the flow of orders to the warehouse, and pre-positioned in state warehouses items such as personal computers whose demand could be forecasted.

---

Exhibit 11.3.  A Faster PC: From Warehouse to Desk Top.

thereby slowing the process and rolling up costs. For example, a survey of state, county, and municipal procurement officials found that, on average, it takes one month or more from receipt of a requisition to the award of a contract (not including the time needed to complete specifications or for delivery), even on many small purchases (National Institute of Governmental Purchasing, 1993).

Reforms to eliminate red tape and help improve procurement performance include:

• *Pruning procedural requirements.* A dramatically simplified system would rely on two broad procedural requirements: (1) written justification for each procurement decision and (2) multiple-member evaluation panels to reach decisions using consensus-based decision processes.

• *Easing requirements on small purchases.* Procedures for making small purchases should be simplified. For example, federal procurement reforms lifted most regulations on purchases of less than $2,500 and raised the threshold for the use of simplified acquisition procedures from $25,000 to $100,000.

• *Using credit cards.* Agencies should be authorized to use commercial purchasing cards for smaller purchases. The federal government's move to purchasing cards will save about $50 in administrative costs for each transaction of $2,500 or less (Shoop, 1994, p. 69).

• *Tapping into electronic commerce.* Computerizing some procurement processes can cut costs, spur competition, speed delivery, and open new opportunities for small businesses (see Exhibit 11.4). In an electronic commerce system, suppliers list products and prices in computer data banks with agencies, enabling them to electronically order the lowest-price item that meets their needs. These systems support initiatives to devolve more flexibility and authority for procurement

---

Oregon's Vendor Information Program (VIP) was the country's first fully automated bid access and purchasing information system (Johnson, 1994). Through the system, businesses can view, download, and print complete bids, attachments, terms and conditions, addenda, and historical bid information. Accessible twenty-four hours per day and seven days per week, VIP catalogues current contract opportunities, lists vendors, and provides up-to-date contract award information. The system, which cost less than $400,000, saved the state over $13,000,000 in its first year of operation.

Exhibit 11.4.    Oregon's Vendor Information Program (VIP).

to line agencies and staffs, while cutting administrative costs and promoting price-value competition among vendors.

# DECENTRALIZE MORE RESPONSIBILITY

When authority for the procurement of low cost and standardized goods is shared or devolved to front-line managers and staff, the unique expertise and experience of centralized purchasing units can be focused on larger, more complex, and costly procurements. In fact, two-thirds of the state, county, and local government procurement agencies responding to a 1993 survey indicated that purchasing is partially decentralized (see Exhibit 11.5). In these systems, procurement responsibility for certain commodities and services is the responsibility of user agencies (National Institute of Governmental Purchasing, 1993).

# STRESS A SERVICE-ORIENTED APPROACH

In a revamped system, centralized procurement offices and officials should be judged on how well they meet the needs and priorities of line agencies and other customers. And as flexibility is granted and some authority is devolved to line agencies for buying needed goods and services, central procurement offices will be called upon to shoulder new roles.

New York's Center for Technology in Government designs, tests, and refines prototype technology systems before state agencies have to commit the resources and political capital to adopt them on a larger scale (Steinbach, 1995a). Each pilot project is a partnership among government, technology corporations, and university faculty and students. Center projects have included applying digital technology to speed the property development permitting process in the six-million-acre Adirondack Park. The University at Albany/SUNY Center also designed

---

Minnesota's Striving Toward Excellence in Performance (STEP) initiative aims to eliminate the barriers created when headquarters staff insists that they know better than front-line agency staff how best to purchase equipment. Under STEP, procurement staff view line managers as their customers. It redefines how the constraints every government agency must work under—fiscal integrity, economical purchase practices, fair employee supervision—are managed. As a result, line agencies have more authority and staff agencies have less.

---

**Exhibit 11.5.    Step Forward in Minnesota.**

a voice recognition and response system to help answer the thirty-five-thousand business start-up questions the state receives each year.

## SUPPORT IMPROVEMENTS WITH TRAINING

More resources and attention must be reserved for educating and training procurement officials and others in the agency's workforce who take on new tasks. The procurement officials' efforts at oversight, information exchange, and accumulation of the lessons learned as experience grows with changes to traditional procurement practices will also expand.

The Philadelphia-based Defense Personnel Support Center supplies food, medical supplies, and clothing to the U.S. military (Steinbach, 1995b). In the past, they have followed an all-too-familiar pattern of military procurement: elaborate specs, contractors, huge stockpiles of aging paraphernalia in large warehouses, and outraged press accounts of waste. Threatened with extinction, the center's employees led the revolution to modernize antiquated practices. Their tools included customer service standards, electronic procurement, and just-in-time inventory. Now, a shared production system with private manufacturers allows the agency to turn around huge priority orders in record time. During Operation Desert Storm, for example, the center delivered one hundred thousand uniforms to Kuwait in less than four weeks.

## IMPROVE PROCUREMENT PROTEST, APPEALS, AND CONFLICT RESOLUTION PROCESSES

Government procurement has become increasingly adversarial and litigious. For example, one-third of the major contracts awarded for information technology buys by the federal government were protested. Increasing the use of alternative dispute resolution techniques such as using third-party, neutral agents in negotiating resolutions or increasing reliance on arbitration should help cut the time and expense involved when grievances cannot be avoided.

But the best remedy could be prevention. Providing wider access to information about bid requests, evaluation processes, and the reasons for selecting the winning bid has helped to drastically cut protests and appeals in Wisconsin's purchases of computer and information technology. On the federal level, agencies will also be required to provide debriefings to unsuccessful bidders detailing how award decisions were reached.

# ENHANCE ENFORCEMENT AGAINST FRAUD AND ABUSE

Tools for monitoring, evaluating, and enforcing bars to fraud and abuse are already plentiful in most procurement systems. Where needed, the authority and resources necessary to safeguard against abuses of the system can be expanded. Establishing a core oversight procurement authority to ensure the integrity of a more flexible and decentralized procurement system, coupled with increased criminal penalties, would also serve to maintain the probity of the system and accountability to the public (see Exhibit 11.6).

---

A task force appointed by Governor John Engler in 1991 reviewed state government purchasing and procurement. The task force's review culminated in numerous recommendations. Key elements of the new purchasing and procurement strategies include (National Governors' Association, 1993, p. 75):

- Restructuring the bidding process to make it more responsive and less expensive
- Revising the organizational structures of purchasing to eliminate steps and empower departments to make the right decisions
- Changing the approach to managing contracts
- Taking paper out of the process

Proposed changes in the bidding process involve:

*Master contract:* Contracts that serve a greater number of agencies reduce the number of procurements and increase the likelihood of getting better prices due to economies of scale

*Partnerships:* In limited circumstances, existing contractors are well suited to perform the work, and it is obvious that their prices are competitive. Rather than conducting new procurements, existing contracts are amended through negotiation with successful vendors.

*Best value:* Purchasing is often based on the lowest bid; life cycle costs and quality factors must be considered in selecting vendors. Procurement decisions should be made based on best value, not low price.

*Problem described, not the solution:* Requests for quotations usually specify a solution. The state should instead release a request for proposals describing the problem and asking vendors to propose a solution and price.

*Acquisition flexibility:* Consider approaches such as competitive negotiations, best and final offers, and techniques that do not specify the evaluation criteria in advance but justify the decision after it is made.

---

**Exhibit 11.6. Michigan Adopts Comprehensive Procurement Plan.**

# —ᴡᴡ— Conclusion

Throughout this book we have stressed that creating high-performance organizations is not a linear process. Change can start like a seed, sprouting anywhere within the organization, and it can grow where it finds conditions to nurture and support it. The only constant is that someone must initiate or become the catalyst for change. Someone must be convinced about the need for better performance and better results.

## INITIATING CHANGE

Public cynicism and frustration with government have led to several legislative and policy developments that may provide catalysts for high-performance organizations. From the enactment of the Government Performance and Results Act to welfare reform legislation, federal, state, and local agencies are being swept into the accountability-for-results wave. From the Clinton administration's National Performance Review to radical government reinvention revolutions in Australia and New Zealand, governments today are now part of a global movement that has been described by many as a new era of public management. Public sector organizations here and around the world are learning that failing to continuously improve quality, control costs, and ensure desired results can forfeit their right or authority to do so. Some other organization will provide the service, and a program or some other entity may be created to take over management functions. The appointment of a control board and the subsequent loss of mayoral authority over several agencies in Washington, D.C., is a dramatic illustration of this trend. Although anyone can stimulate change, today's performance- and results-focused climate may make it easier to promote needed changes and ultimately to engage top-level management in the process.

## Meeting Key Requirements

This book has presented the requirements for creating high-performance organizations. These include

Sustained leadership focused on high performance

Willingness to develop performance measures

Willingness to eventually change whole organizations to provide quality and more appropriate services at equal or reduced costs

Willingness to allocate resources to continuous learning at all levels within the organization

The first requirement—sustained leadership—is not unique to creating high-performance organizations. Every change process depends on leadership, to some degree. The style of leadership in high-performance entities is unique, and related leadership skills depart from those that characterize traditional hierarchical organizations. Leaders of high-performance organizations must be creative, flexible, politically savvy, resilient, and extremely good communicators or facilitators of dialogue. Yes, anyone with these qualities (at any level) within the organization can start the process. Top-level management must ultimately be drawn in, however.

Organizational success depends on leadership's capacity to generate the willingness to participate and to grow among front-line employees as well as management. Leadership must also be somewhat transparent, which means becoming more vulnerable. And high-performance leadership is shared leadership. Team dynamics are common. The people acting as catalysts for change to a high-performance approach may not envision themselves as leaders, yet they must soon see several others sharing or embracing the change concepts. The performance infection must spread throughout the department, and ultimately the agency, if it is to succeed.

The remaining requirements for high-performance organizations are more unique to this type of organizational change. Although they have been discussed at length throughout the chapters of the book, some important lessons will be emphasized in the sections that follow.

## Developing Performance Measures

Critical lessons about developing performance measures are beginning to emerge from state and local government experiments of the last decade. Oregon reduced their number of benchmarks (performance indicators) dramatically. More is not always better. Innovators in California learned from service providers that incremental indicators, which reflected steps needed to reach a goal, could be defined as benchmarks. Milestones reached within the GED program were as important as completion of the program. Finally, high-performance organizations use benchmarks or indicators to learn more about agency needs and processes.

As such, they must not be used solely as leverage for assessing or motivating employee performance. Failure to achieve an outcome may be the best indicator of the need for better information systems or for more marketing resources. Involving direct-service providers or front-line workers in establishing indicators is also a vital lesson. Employees are more willing to be held accountable for measures they have defined. This area provides an opportunity for creating new labor-management partnerships. Workers and their representatives can work together to create realistic performance measures.

In public sector organizations, the willingness to develop performance measures must often be coupled with a change in perspective about the nature of performance. Public sector organizations must move away from the more traditional focus on *activities* or *services provided,* toward quantifiable results, outcomes, and impact. For example, a performance indicator would change from the hours of counseling services provided to the number of children now in permanent homes through adoption.

Quantifiable performance measures may require innovations in data collection and tracking technology. Performance measures will also be influenced by the available baseline data or information. Despite these implications and challenges, innovators must work to avoid the tendency to escape quantifying results by talking about simply improving or increasing outcomes. Changes in performance should be measurable.

## Changing Whole Organizations

Just as creating measurable indicators to assess performance has implications in terms of information and data systems, the move to becoming a high-performance organization will change the whole organization and affect all its key operations and relationships. There will be changes in the relationships between people and their work. The relationship between the organization and its customers will change. And finally, the relationship between organizations and their external citizens or stakeholders will change. These changes are the transition signature of results-driven, high-performance organizations.

Whole-organization change is clearly about human interactions and therefore is a complex process. Change will usually be gradual and will be built on a solid foundation that establishes a clear sense of purpose within a realistic environmental context. This foundation process engages representatives of all the needed stakeholders creating widespread commitment to change throughout the organization. Only after this deliberate groundwork has been laid can the whole-organization change be considered feasible. Constant feedback and patience are most critical. Employees must have a clear sense of where they are and how they are doing if they are to motivate and engage others. Incentives and recognition of success become useful tools.

Using citizen-as-customer feedback mechanisms has been a valuable tool in cities like Hampton, Virginia, and Phoenix, Arizona. Customer-feedback strategies provide on-the-spot ways for motivating performance and troubleshooting about related systems and processes.

## Allocating Resources to Continuous Learning

Getting an organization to a point where all parties share the commitment and the responsibility for high performance requires a willingness to invest in the learning needs of individuals while becoming more people-centered. High-performance organizations rely on highly and multiply skilled individuals who have the capacity to change and to continuously develop in new ways. Specialists may have to become generalists. Tasks change rapidly, and employees need to retool for new roles. The training and HRM department can form the skeletal frame upon which the transition to high performance rests. Human resource teams must participate as part of the organizational redesign process. They have important insights about the structure, features, tools, technology, people, values, and information and decision systems of the organization. Failure to engage HRM is costly and can sabotage the best-intentioned efforts.

It is important to distinguish between training and learning. High-performance organizations are learning organizations. Managers, employees, stakeholders, and customers express a willingness to continue to expand their understanding and capacities. This is a participatory concept. Training connotes one-way, one-time, or event-centered information transfer. Learning, however, may include well-designed training experiences. It also may include coaching, mentoring, support, and team application, as well as problem solving. Resources must be built into the plan to support and to integrate systems for continual learning.

## Monitoring Your Progress

Once these requirements have been met, you can tell if your public sector agency is becoming a high-performance organization if you can answer yes to the following questions:

Do you now have better, more effective quantifiable measures of performance or results?

Do you have or are you creating ways to assess and measure improvements in performance?

Do you have well-understood measures of the internal characteristics, culture, and systems of your agency?

Do you have systematic measures of citizen, customer, and stakeholder perceptions?

Are you clear about the purpose of your organization? Do you think everyone is?

Can you state (in quantifiable terms) how well you are doing in achieving stated goals?

## Translating Private Sector Concepts

If public agencies continue to create high-performance organizations in response to environmental, legislative, and conscience demands, they will probably continue to look to the private sector for direction in this results-driven, performance-based revolution. This book has been careful to distinguish the public from the private sector. Government agencies and products are usually less tangible than private sector products and services; certainly, customers may be less obvious. There may be political risks or unintended consequences associated with attempts to engage public sector customers. In addition, public agencies have historically emphasized processes such as caseloads, services, available units of housing, or numbers of police or probation officers.

Shifting to a result and outcome focus is a prerequisite for creating high-performance public sector organizations. This shift, however, may be the most problematic challenge. Elected and appointed officials are subject to the pressures of elections and campaign mandates. Long-term investments and developmental frameworks of high-performance organizations often conflict with short-term political realities. Despite these constraints, public agencies now face unparalleled opportunities for creating high-performance organizations; and benchmarks can be designed and communicated in "election proof" ways. More dramatically, benchmarks and results can be framed in compelling and inclusive terms, thereby engaging opposing factions. Conservatives and liberals can often agree on outcomes, if not processes. Performance measures may create occasions for collaboration because they emphasize the desired results. In domestic policy issues, these results often relate to quality-of-life matters, about which debate is limited. Reduced crime, stable families, and safer water are shared values. Public agencies will need to be strategic as they work to become more results-oriented, however. Innovators must recognize that elected or appointed officials will weigh political realities and timing issues in their decisions.

On the plus side, the inclusive whole-organizational dynamics associated with creating high-performance organizations may help elected officials overcome some of the obstacles and resistance commonly faced during transitions from one administration to another. If stakeholders, employees, management, and citizens-customers are all marching to the same (or a similar) drummer, continuity for results is easier to achieve.

The catalyst for change within public agencies must find and build consensus about analogs to private sector concepts such as customers, services, products, and customer satisfaction or to profit-and-loss issues before trying to create benchmarks and performance indicators. This translation of the private sector culture to the public world is critical.

Sometimes, this translation emerges when the vision, mission, and values are more clearly defined. Once agreement is reached about what your organization is trying to do, what the preferred future is, what it accomplishes (with others, usually), and what its attributes and operational commitments are, it may be easier to clarify analogs to private sector concepts. Customers and services become clearer.

In high-performance organizations the visioning process, which includes crafting a mission and determining guiding principles and values, is not an annual or every-five-year exercise for top management. It must somehow involve the whole organization (and others from outside the agency) and be transmitted to and reinforced throughout the workplace and organizational community continuously. The big picture must be understood and shared by all.

This infusion of the big picture throughout the organization fuels the needed culture change. Culture is the sum total of the ways in which an organization operates and works together. It is the sum total of relationships, specifically the nature and quality of these relationships.

## Regrouping and Going Forward

Resilience will characterize individuals who choose to work in high-performance organizations. They will know that failure is part of the process. When benchmarks are not achieved, team members must regroup and go forward. Given all the complexities and challenges of moving public sector organizations from the old to the new, from a process to a results focus, an African proverb seems appropriate. Innovators would be wise to remember that "to stumble is not to fall but to move forward faster."

As our society emerges from the industrial age, we no longer can question whether or not we should create high-performance organizations. It is rapidly becoming a matter of when the shift will occur. For individuals, the question is, With which high-performance organization will I affiliate and in what ways?

The insights, tools, and resources presented in this book are designed to help make the transition process less stressful for public sector agencies, thereby increasing the probability that you will succeed in creating and functioning in high-performance organizations.

# ⎯ᴧᴧ⎯ References

American Federation of Labor-Congress of Industrial Organizations. *Reinvigorating the Public Service: Strengthening the Link Between Pay and Performance.* Washington, D.C.: American Federation of Labor-Congress of Industrial Organizations, 1991.

Angle, M. "Fewer Rules May Curb Procurement Abuses." *Congressional Quarterly,* Mar. 12, 1994, *52*(10), 638.

Applebaum, E., and Batt, R. *The New American Workplace: Transforming Work Systems in the United States.* Ithaca, N.Y.: ILR Press, 1994.

Barnett, C. C. "Redesigning Austin's Health Clinics." *The Public Innovator,* 1994, *14,* pp. 1–2.

Brizius, J. *Deciding for Investment.* Washington, D.C.: Alliance for Redesigning Government, 1994.

Brizius, J. A., and Campbell, M. D. *Getting Results.* Washington, D.C.: Council of Governors' Policy Advisors, 1991.

Bruner, C., with Scott, S., and Stekette, M. W. *Potential Returns on Investment from a Comprehensive Family Center Approach in High-Risk Allegheny County Neighborhoods.* University of Pittsburgh Office of Child Development Family Support Policy Board, Feb. 1996.

Campbell, M. D., and Foster, S. E. *Prerequisites for Developing a Performance Management System, from a Review of the Oregon and Texas Experience in Building Performance Measurement and Reporting Systems, Data Selection, Collection and Reporting.* Washington, D.C.: National Institute for Literacy, 1995.

Caudle, S. *Reengineering for Results.* Washington, D.C.: National Academy of Public Administration, 1994.

Chapman-Welch, W. "Talking Management." *The Washington Post,* Mar. 23, 1997, p. H1.

Chynoweth, J. K., and Dyer, B. R. *Strengthening Families: A Guide for State Policymaking.* Washington, D.C.: Council of Governors' Policy Advisors, 1991.

Creech, B. *The Five Pillars of TQM.* New York.: Truman Talley Books (Dutton), 1994.

Delaney, G. "Managing Public Budgets." Unpublished presentation materials, 1995.

Finkle, E. "Educational Support Agency Buys in Bulk." *The Public Innovator,* 1995a, *30,* pp. 3–4.

Finkle, E. "Performance Measurement Minefield." *The Public Innovator,* 1995b, *43,* pp. 1–2.

Finkle, E. "Pushing Authority and Dollars to the Classroom." *The Public Innovator,* 1995c, *20,* pp. 2–3.

Finkle, E. "Restructure, Or Else." *The Public Innovator,* 1995d, *25,* pp. 1–2.

Finkle, E. "San Jose Plans for Strategic Change." *The Public Innovator,* 1995e, *33,* p. 5.

Friar, M. E., and Leonard, H. B. *The Federal Budget and the States: Fiscal Year 1993.* Cambridge, Mass: Taubman Center for State and Local Government, John F. Kennedy School of Government, Harvard University, 1994.

Friedman, M. "Results Based Decision Making and Budgeting." Discussion Materials, Fiscal Policy Studies Institute, Baltimore, 1996.

Fruchter, S. "Reinvention and Strategic Planning at NOAA." Unpublished remarks by Sue Fruchter at Learning from the Leaders: Alliance Working Seminar, Aug. 8, 1995.

Galbraith, J. R., and Lawler, E. E., III. *Organizations for the Future: The New Logic for Managing Complex Organizations.* San Francisco: Jossey-Bass, 1995.

George, S. *Total Quality Management.* New York: Wiley, 1994.

Hammer, M., and Champy, J. *Reengineering the Corporation,* New York: HarperBusiness, 1993.

Hulick, C. "Buying Smarter." *The Public Innovator,* 1995, *34/35,* p. 5.

International Personnel Management Association, Federal Section. *Labor Management Relations in the Federal Government: Can It be Reinvented?* Washington, D.C.: International Personnel Management Association, Federal Section, 1993.

Johnson, N. "Buying Smarter." *The Public Innovator,* 1994, *3,* pp. 2–3.

Johnson, W. B., Faul, S., Huang, B., and Packer, A. H. *Civil Service 2000.* Washington, D.C.: U.S. Government Printing Office, 1988.

Kelman, S. *Procurement and Public Management: The Fear of Discretion and the Quality of Public Performance.* Washington, D.C.: AEI Press, 1990.

Kravetz, D. *The Human Resources Revolution.* San Francisco: Jossey-Bass, 1988.

Lacey, R. *Ford: The Men and the Machine.* Boston: Little, Brown, 1986.

Leonard, B., Cook, J., and McNeil, J. "The Role of Budget and Financial Reform in Making Government Work Better and Cost Less." *Public Budgeting and Financing,* Spring 1995, *15,* pp. 1–12.

Macy, C. H. *The Oregon Option: A Federal-State-Local Partnership for Better Results.* Baltimore: The Annie E. Casey Foundation, 1997.

Maymi, C. Presentation to Learning from the Leaders: Alliance Working Seminar, Washington, D.C., Aug. 8, 1995.

Miller, G. J. "Productivity and the Budget Process." In M. Holzer (ed.), *Public Productivity Handbook.* New York: Dekker, 1992.

Mohrman, A. M., Jr., Resnick-West, S. M., and Lawler, E. E., III. *Designing Performance Appraisal Systems: Aligning Appraisals and Organizational Realities.* San Francisco: Jossey-Bass, 1990.

Narcisso, A. "Municipal Performance Measurement: Mixed But Encouraging Signs." *The Public Innovator,* 1996, *53,* pp. 3–5.

National Academy of Public Administration. *Modernizing Federal Classification: An Opportunity for Excellence.* Washington, D.C.: National Academy of Public Administration, 1991.

National Academy of Public Administration. *Leading People in Change: Empowerment, Commitment, Accountability.* Washington, D.C.: National Academy of Public Administration, 1993.

National Academy of Public Administration. *Broad-Banding Literature Review and Bibliography.* Washington, D.C.: National Academy of Public Administration, 1994.

National Academy of Public Administration. *Innovative Approaches to Human Resources Management.* Washington, D.C.: National Academy of Public Administration, 1995a.

National Academy of Public Administration. *Strategies and Alternatives for Redefining Human Resources Management.* Washington, D.C.: National Academy of Public Administration, 1995b.

National Commission on the State and Local Public Service. *Hard Truths/Tough Choices: An Agenda for State and Local Reform.* Albany, N.Y.: The Nelson A. Rockefeller Institute of Government, 1993.

National Governors' Association. *An Action Agenda to Redesign State Government.* Washington, D.C.: National Governors' Association, 1993.

National Institute of Governmental Purchasing. *Interim 1993 Procurement Survey Results: Responses as of July 13, 1994.* Falls Church, Va.: National Institute of Governmental Purchasing, 1993.

National Performance Review. *Creating a Government That Works Better and Costs Less. Reinventing Human Resource Management. Accompanying Report of the National Performance Review.* Washington, D.C.: U.S. Government Printing Office, 1993.

Oregon Economic Development Department. *Oregon Shines: An Economic Strategy for the Pacific Century (Summary).* Salem: Oregon Economic Development Department, 1989.

Oregon Progress Board. *Oregon Benchmarks: 1993 Report to the Legislature.* Salem: Oregon Progress Board, 1993.

Oregon Progress Board. *Oregon Shines II: Updating Oregon's Strategic Plan—A Report to the People of Oregon.* Salem: Oregon Progress Board and The Governor's Oregon Shines Task Force, Jan. 21, 1997.

Osborne, D., and Gaebler, T. *Reinventing Government: How the Entrepreneurial Spirit Is Transforming the Public Sector.* Reading, Mass.: Addison-Wesley, 1992.

Parkhurst, D. "Success of Government Services Principles." *The Public Innovator,* 1994, 6, p. 5.

Popovich, M. G. "Labor-Management Cooperation: Win-Win a Win." *The Public Innovator,* 1994, 9, pp. 1–2.

Popovich, M. G. "SNAP Into Action: Chicago." *The Public Innovator,* 1995, 27, pp. 2–3.

Popovich, M. G. *Toward Results-Oriented Intergovernmental Systems: An Historical Look at the Development of the Oregon Benchmarks.* Washington, D.C.: Alliance for Redesigning Government, 1996.

Posner, B. G., and Rothstein, L. R. "Reinventing the Business of Government: An Interview with Change Catalyst David Osborne." *Harvard Business Review,* May-June 1994, pp. 132–143.

Resnick-West, S. *Managing Change to TQM.* Houston, Tex.: Association for Quality and Participation, 1993.

Resnick-West, S. *Benchmarking Worksheet.* Resnick-West Consulting, 1994.

Rosenberg, J. "Redesigning Budget Systems: Deciding for Investment Budgeting." *The Public Innovator,* 1994, 11, pp. 3–4.

Schilder, D. E., Brady, A., and Horsch, K. *Resource Guide of Results-Based Accountability Efforts: Profiles of Selected States.* Cambridge, Mass.: Harvard Family Research Project, 1996.

Shoop, T. "Steven Kelman: Advocate of Reform." *Government Executive,* Aug. 1994, 26(8), pp. 68–72.

State and Local Government Labor-Management Committee. *Labor Management Cooperation in Today's Workplace: Case Studies from the Sixth National Labor Management Conference.* Washington, D.C.: State and Local Government Labor-Management Committee, May 1992.

Steinbach, C. "Local, State, and Federal Innovations." *The Public Innovator,* 1995a, *34/35,* pp. 1–2.

Steinbach, C. "More Federal Innovations." *The Public Innovator,* 1995b, *36,* pp. 4–5.

Stone, B. "Works Better, Costs Less: The National Performance Review." Remarks at Learning from the Leaders: Alliance for Redesigning Government Working Seminar, Washington, D.C., Aug. 8, 1995.

Sturdivant, J. Remarks at National Academy of Public Administration Brown Bag Seminar, Washington, D.C., Sept. 24, 1994.

U.S. Department of Commerce. *Survey of Current Business,* July 1988, *68.*

U.S. General Accounting Office. *Effectively Implementing the Government Performance and Results Act.* U.S. General Accounting Office/ GGD–96–118. Washington, D.C.: Government Printing Office, 1996.

Widner, M. "Iowa Quality Government." Presentation to The Policymakers Institute, St. Louis, Mo., sponsored by the Danforth Foundation, Aug. 1996.

# ~ Index

CPSIA information can be obtained
at www.ICGtesting.com
Printed in the USA
JSHW041918151220
10298JS00001B/2

9 780787 941024